The
Slowest Pilgrim

Harry Townsend

The Slowest Pilgrim

published in Great Britain by
Dreamtime Publications
6 Manor Road
East Grinstead
West Sussex
RH19 1LR
England

A catalogue record of this book is available from the British Library

ISBN
0-9554396-0-4
978-0-9554396-0-5

Typesetting and printing: David Brown Maynards Green 01435 812506

Contents

Acknowledgements

I want to thank everybody that I met along the Camino for their support and friendship: it's a wonderful self supporting 'family', with everybody looking out for each other yet without intruding on each other's space.

Thanks also to the Confraternity of St James, 27 Blackfriars Road, London, SE1 8NY www.csj.org.uk who make it possible for everybody to walk the Camino in safety and (relative) comfort. Their guidebooks and other publications are invaluable: their friendship and support is limitless.

Enormous thanks to David Brown, whose encouragement, enthusiasm and vast knowledge of publishing transformed my naïve typescript into a presentable book.

Finally, thanks to family and friends for just being there: they are everything to me.

Foreword

Being a gardener, sunshine has always gladdened my heart. When I wake from a good night's sleep and see the sun slanting in through the window my spirits rise. But I've also become aware, over the years, of the dangers of too much sun, with melanoma doubling every ten years, and affecting 1 in 50 people in Britain. With a high death rate and no guaranteed cure, it's one of the fastest growing cancers.

I used to work with Harry Townsend at Kew when I was Supervisor of Staff Training and he had the exalted rank of Assistant Curator. I remember, too, his wife Myfanwy for her bright personality and her wonderful voice – she was a fine singer and a memorable 'Eliza' in a production of *My Fair Lady*. So it's with mixed feelings of both regret and hope that I urge you to support the charity that Harry and his sons have established in Myfanwy's memory – the Myfanwy Townsend Melanoma Research Fund (www.melanoma-fund.co.uk). It is dedicated to the vital task of funding research to find a cure, raise awareness and make diagnosis more readily available.

Much as we all love the sunshine, we need to do more to make sure that we can enjoy it in safety. If Myfanwy's fund can achieve that, it will bring back a smile to the faces of all who knew her, and make our future all the brighter.

Alan Titchmarsh MBE

What's It All About?

When my wife Myfanwy died on October 20th 1999 from the skin cancer malignant melanoma, myself and our three sons Mark, Stewart and Cameron set up a (properly registered) Charity, the Myfanwy Townsend Melanoma Research Fund, www.melanoma-fund.co.uk, Charity Registration number 1085969.

Our objectives were to raise awareness, and to support research to strive to find a cure for this terrible disease from which more than a million people alive today in Britain will suffer.

The death rate from malignant melanoma is 25%.

The incidence is far higher in Australia, and even higher in New Zealand.

The seed firm Thompson and Morgan has produced a sweet pea named Myfanwy Townsend, of which we have sold many thousands of packets to date, whilst Leeds United Football Club are a major supporter.

Their Sports Therapist Bruce Craven died aged only 32 from melanoma, and the players donated from their own pockets to establish the lime green wristbands with the words MELANOMA AWARENESS www.melanoma-fund.co.uk

We also do many fund raising 'Challenges' to raise money.

I'm 67: I've climbed Mount Kilimanjaro with our youngest son Cameron and brother in law Peter Clarke, run the Death Valley Marathon, 'rowed' a marathon (42,195m) on a rowing machine in the gym, and trekked the Grand Canyon from Rim to

Rim non-stop with the entire front row of the rugby club that I was coaching (Gary Hall, Jim Canavan, Ted Morris and Ted's wife Carol, with Malcolm Garrett-Eynon as support crew).

This is the story of my most recent 'Challenge', walking the Pilgrim Trail, the Camino, from St Jean Pied de Port in France across the Pyrenees to Santiago de Compostela in north west Spain, 760 km in 38 days, and of the amazing people that I met and their often even more amazing stories.

Was it successful?

Read it and find out: but I'll give you a clue, it wouldn't have been a book worth writing if I'd stopped walking the Camino half way!

Harry Townsend

Spanish Pilgrim Trail

I (Harry Townsend) set out from St Jean Pied de Port on July 19th 2003 to walk the 760 km (475 miles) of the Pilgrim Trail (the Camino Francés) to the Shrine of St James at Santiago de Compostela.

It had been intended as a sponsored walk to raise money for the Charity that we set up in memory of my wife, the Myfanwy Townsend Melanoma Research Fund: it became one of the greatest experiences of my adventurous life!

The Camino, as it is known, has been walked by hundreds of thousands of pilgrims for more than a thousand years: they walked from their homes throughout Europe.

No cheap coaches, or trains, or cut price airlines to whisk you back home in those days: you simply turned round at Santiago – and walked home again!

It was so hazardous that all made their wills before setting out.

Almost half never returned.

Many were already sick, and died along the way: some were attacked by robbers, some killed by wolves, some set up other lives.

Walking the Camino was incredibly hard, and a series of Hospitals, Hostals and Refuges where pilgrims could stay overnight was set up by the Church along the route and are still the basis of the Refugios (Refuges) and Albergues where the modern pilgrims (up to 25,000 a year) shelter each night.

You get a bunk (two, or occasionally three-tier bunks) in unisex dormitories with a mattress and very often a pillow: toilets, wash basins, showers (some faintly warm), kitchen facilities (sometimes) and a basic sink with rubbing board and cold water to wash your clothes.

Inhibitions vanish rapidly!

All for between €3 and €5 a night (£2 to £3).

When you reach Santiago, you can obtain your certificate (Compostela).

This is granted to any who have walked the final 100 km, or cycled or ridden on horseback the final 200 km, in one continuous journey.

Horse riders are rare, however: didn't meet one personally, but they do exist.

Many present-day pilgrims will have taken several years over the journey from St Jean Pied de Port or from Roncesvalles, taking a week of their holidays each year.

But I wanted to complete what is regarded as a major Challenge, the entire 760 km walk in one journey.

So I stayed overnight in the Albergue at St Jean Pied de Port in France: and at 0540 on the morning of July 19th 2003, I started the long journey, crossing the Pyrenees in to Spain on the first day to the monastery at Roncesvalles with a 38 days walk ahead (no rest days!) to finish on August 25th at the cathedral in Santiago de Compostela.

Pilgrims must carry their Pilgrim Passport (their *Credencial*) to gain access to the Refuges: this is stamped (a 'stamp' is called a *sello*), signed and dated at every Refuge, and at many churches, town halls and even bars (best not to have too many of the latter, though!) and makes a wonderful colourful record of your journey to Santiago.

If you have an unbroken sequence of these (often very decorative) stamps over a period of at least 100 km (for walkers) or 200 km (for cyclists and riders), you may be granted your *Compostela*, or Certificate of Pilgrimage, in recognition of your achievement and motivation in following the Camino, when you present your Pilgrim Record (Pilgrim Passport) at the cathedral's Pilgrim Office or Secretariat: and you'll know that you have earned the right to wear the conch shell, the emblem of St James, which most pilgrims carry proudly along the Camino.

I'm incredibly proud to wear mine, especially after having earned it over not just 100 km but over almost 800 km.

I am thumbing through my Pilgrim Passport as I write: 58 stamps (*sellos*) which bring so many memories!

Pilgrim Passports can be obtained from the Pilgrim Record Secretary at the Confraternity of St James, 27 Blackfriars Road, London, SE1 8NY (www.csj.org.uk): and in any case, if you intend to walk the Camino, you should become a member.

They'll be delighted to welcome you: and they can provide enormous help and advice!

Alternatively, Pilgrim Passports can be obtained at many places along the Camino: the Accueil St. Jacques in St Jean Pied de Port, for instance, or the Monastery at Roncesvalles amongst others.

Another thing that the aspiring pilgrim will need is the *Pilgrim Guide to Spain*: it was invaluable to me! This can also be obtained from the Confraternity of St James.

So that's another reason to join!

I met pilgrims from every corner of the world, who were walking the Camino for such a vast variety of reasons: Japan, Brazil (I met Marco, who had nourished the idea of walking the Camino for fifteen years 'to find the Truth'), Spain of course, France, Italy, England, Ireland, Portugal, many from Germany, Sweden, Slovenia, USA, Canada… the list is endless, and we all became friends as we shared the hardships.

The trail is well waymarked with red and white flashes (in the early stages), or a golden stylised shell on a blue background, and latterly with yellow arrows, painted on walls and roads, signposts, kilometre markers and many times with special symbols: it is a unique walk over trails, tracks, minor and occasionally major roads through villages and occasionally towns and even cities. Everywhere, the pilgrim (Peregrino) is welcomed and helped: they are so much a part of life along the Camino.

I used two trekking poles, which take a lot of the strain, and carried my rucksack (best if you can find a light framed one, that lets the small of your back 'breathe'), sleeping bag (one season), sleeping mat (you will need it, if you are too late to get a bunk at often overstretched Refuges), basic washing equipment for self and clothes, a single change of clothes, a towel, flip flops or sandals (to wear in the Refuges), the essential guide books, medical equipment, clothes pegs, a waterproof (although, fortunately, I met rain only for an hour on the last morning, this can be a hazard particularly during the last few days across Galicia) and the **big** essential, water containers.

It was mid-summer: but just in case, a **thin** fleece can be a good idea!

Even so, this weighed more than 12 kg: and that was **after** I sent 3 kg of unwanted clothing etc. back home from Pamplona.

This is such a frequent occurrence that the man at the Post

Office didn't even smile: just reached the usual box down from the shelf!

I did some cooking, but it was easier (and even cheaper!) to get a Menu Peregrino (Pilgrim's Meal) that almost every café/bar or restaurant along the Camino offers.

Three courses, including wine and bread, for between €5.5 and €8 (£3.50 to £5): you can't grumble at **that**!

It's too heavy to carry cooking equipment, of course: you carry some food, and hope that the kitchens that you find at many Refuges will have enough pots, pans, plates and utensils.

Many do.

Not a bad idea to carry a knife, fork, spoon and plastic mug, though.

You'll also often find food 'donated' by earlier pilgrims: consume this with caution!

You try to start by 06.00 and to complete the day's walk by midday, or at the latest by 1300: because after that, the temperature is well into the 100°F range and in fact, at Logroño, it was still 104°F at almost six o'clock in the evening.

The sun is at your back through most of your walking day.

Three major mountains to cross: the Pyrenees, the Cruz de Ferro (almost 5,000 ft), then the feared O Cebreiro, a five hour demanding climb from the wonderful little Refuge at Ruitelán.

You have to cross the Meseta, the wheat producing lands across the centre of northern Spain, for a week. Flat, no shade anywhere, the road stretches in a straight line into the distance between the empty yellow wheat fields, with the temperature reaching the usual 100°F by 09.30 or 10.00, and sweat drenching you for three or more hours until you fall in to your shady bunk at the Refuge (**after** having washed your clothes, because if you don't make it your first priority, there will be no room on the washing lines, and **after** having tried to get a fairly warm shower!).

Got to get your priorities right: wash clothes first, self second!

Oh yes: forgot to mention, the Meseta is followed by the Páramo, which is also flat, but bleaker: and then comes the Maragatería, which is mountainous and very barren. The good news is, it only lasts for about 30 miles.

Then comes Galicia, with it's green lanes winding up and down steep hills: and if you're going to meet rain anywhere along the Camino, this is where you'll meet it!

You walk down, up, down and up....then down, and up.... and down and up again.... the steep Galician 'green lanes' (no Spanish hill counts unless it lasts for at least 3 km!) to the last major peak, the Alto de Poio.

But there's lots more long sharp climbs after that: they're just as punishing, but not so high!

The Camino, if you want to follow it on the map, goes through Estella, Logroño, Nájera, Santo Domingo de la Calzada, Burgos, Castrojeriz, Fromista, Carrión de los Condes, Sahagún, León, Astorga, Ponferrada, Villafranca, Cebreiro, Sarria and Melide to Santiago de Compostela in the north west corner of Spain, close to Finisterre which in mediaeval times was thought to be the end of the known world.

These are all towns through which we as a family used to drive in our Commer dormobile every May more than thirty years ago when I was plant collecting in the remote mountain areas of central Spain for Kew Gardens and the British Museum.

The area is a hotbed of history: and the churches and cathedrals in the towns and cities are so magnificent as to be undescribable in simple words.

I felt such a wonderful sense of achievement when I reached Santiago de Compostela after 38 days non-stop walking (no rest days!) and received my Compostela: so many of us had been together day after day, not walking together necessarily, but meeting and eating at Refugios (refuges) night after night, and supporting each other through the long days of the Camino.

It was like 'the last day of term' when we all reached Santiago separately, and then met up in the huge square outside the magnificent cathedral: and at night, groups of musicians played until well after the warm midnight to large crowds sitting on the steps as we all celebrated our personal achievements.

Sadly, I raised virtually nothing in sponsorship: but the experiences and friendships formed along the Camino made up for this disappointment.

So I'd like to thank some of my many friends (nobody mentions surnames, we only introduce ourselves by our given names): Renata, Dieter, Brighton Boy, Benoit, Maggie, Rachel and Julia (the Gloucester Girls), Francesc, Thomas Named After A Brand of Beer and his wife, Marco, the English Family On A Walking Holiday who lent me a T shirt when I left mine on the line, Ada (who gave me a razor when mine broke), Thomas the Pilgrim, Popeye, Virginia, José Antonio, Itzia….and there are many many more whose names I don't know but whose faces are so well remembered.

I say 'Thank you for your help and friendship' to all of you.

I hope that, if you read this book, you'll tell your friends why I did the walk, and refer them to our website www.melanoma-fund.co.uk which also tells them that we've already donated £23,000 to establish the **Myfanwy Townsend Melanoma Laboratory** within RAFT at Mount Vernon Hospital, Northwood.

If you want to get in touch with me (hope you do!), just e-mail harry@melanoma-fund.co.uk; and if you want to walk the Camino, then (as I said earlier) you should join the Confraternity of St James, 27 Blackfriars Road, London SE1 8NY, www.csj.org.uk .

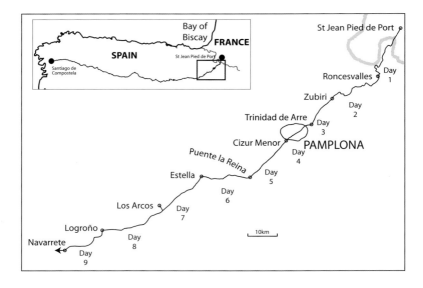

1

Across the Pyrenees and into Spain

Day 1
St Jean Pied de Port to Roncesvalles
26 km   760 km to go

It's all Alison Raju's fault that I carry this burden of guilt.

Her Guide Book, *The Way of St James*, said that there were two ways from St Jean Pied de Port over the Pyrenees to Roncesvalles: by road (where you can't get lost as long as you fork **right** and not **left** at Valcarlos), or over the mountains.

I was rather hoping that the weather might be bad, because she comments 'if the weather is very bad, or visibility poor, you may prefer to take the former', which would have eased my conscience.

But the weather was determinedly good.

Anyway, as a serial taker of the wrong way, who can even take the wrong turning coming back from the shops, I didn't want to lose my way on the very first day high up in the Pyrenees: as nobody would know that I was there in the first place, my chances of being rescued would be slight.

So I walked on the road: and it's tormented me ever since.

Maybe I'll go back and do that stage again some time: or

there again, perhaps I might not…, but it will still bother me, just a little…

I'd arrived at St Jean Pied de Port the previous afternoon, a virgin pilgrim. The Refuge was at the top end of the Rue de la Citadelle, a daunting climb: and sweat dripped onto the desk as I stood in the Information Office, staffed by weekly volunteers who patiently dispensed information and stamped passports.

No, the Refuge didn't open until 4pm: so I sat in the 'garden' and ate a decomposing Sainsbury's cookie.

I was joined by two French youths, who intended to walk the Camino with tent and fishing rods: but they lost interest and wandered down to the river to fish. I never saw them again.

Four o'clock, and I'd been joined by another potential pilgrim ready for the twelve bed dormitory. All that I had to eat was an old baguette. I wandered forlornly round the kitchen, tantalised by the pot of aromatic pasta being whipped up by Jeannine, the Hospitalero, and studiously keeping out of her way as she rattled off a stream of Basque like a machine gun.

She looked strangely like Dick Emery: I kept expecting her to push me against a wall and say 'Ooh, you are awful!'

But what she did say (in French) was 'Would you like to eat with us?'

Would I? You bet I would! It was almost Jeannine's personal Refuge: the pilgrims were her life, her continually enlarging 'family', and she was one of the kindest people imaginable.

She'd already recruited three girls to eat, plus a rotund and reclusive Frenchman who revealed himself as The Human Vacuum Cleaner.

Seconds? The Human Vacuum Cleaner was there: and when it came to scraping the leftovers into the bin, he was there first to sweep the last five scoops on to his plate and retire to a corner with the last fragments of bread.

Out on the patio, the Pyrenees as a majestic backcloth, lay Dieter. He'd walked from the Black Forest: and he'd been resting his inflamed tendons and horribly lacerated feet up against the wall for the past twenty four hours.

Yes, it's his **real** name: although I grant you, I don't **always** mention real names. For instance, I'm pretty sure that The Human Vacuum Cleaner was not his given name. Anyway 'Dieter' rhymes with 'heater': or 'mosquiter' or, well, with lots of things: but it **doesn't** mean somebody who's not eating very much (there we go again, 'eater') hoping to lose weight (on a diet!): although, come to think of it, he didn't seem to eat a great deal. Maybe you're right, after all: perhaps it's what they call 'double entendre' in a very **nice** way (no smut here!)

Three hyper active French youngsters, who'd played themselves in for the previous 500 miles, made up the numbers.

Bed at 9.30: lights out at 10.00.

St Jean Pied de Port:
only 760km to go!

The hyper active French were first to rise at 0430, torches at the ready as they packed their rucksacks and shuffled towards the door. Dieter was also eager to be off: they were all taking the Route Napoleon over the Pyrenees.

I set out at 5.40, striding purposefully down the hill, a trekking pole in either hand, enormous back pack weighing me down. If I didn't hate throwing anything away, I would have jettisoned 50% by the time I reached the bottom of the hill.

I was bitten by my first dog after 2.5 km.

'Don't worry about Spanish dogs, they're pretty lazy,' I'd been told.

Well of course, it was a **French** dog, a cross between a pony and an Alsatian, that bounded out of the farmhouse and made the obligatory threatening noises: and it obviously didn't know that it was just not cricket to bite pilgrims. But there again, perhaps it was the dog's way of making it's own personal comment about pilgrims who went the road way, rather than over the mountains.

Anyway, it had been suggested back home that I should take a personal alarm for such eventualities. The dog quite liked the noise: it tried to seize and swallow it. Now, that would have been interesting: how long would the battery last inside the dog before it ran down? **That** would teach it, not to try to bite pilgrims!

I switched it off, and the dog made a tactical retreat. Whilst I strode away, back turned, it sidled up furtively and clamped it's jaws around the back of my ample thigh. No, it didn't draw blood: but I could certainly feel teeth stapling spare flesh together.

I turned round and shouted at it and waved my trekking poles: ah, that was better, the sort of reaction that it understood, and it gambolled away obviously feeling quite relieved.

The first 8 km to Valcarlos were a rather jolly stroll. I stopped at a garage for a drink and a Kitkat. I asked the girl if we were in

France or Spain.

She wasn't sure, but it was one or the other.

Then the road turned upwards: 18 km of solid, grinding ascent. No pubs, no ice cream vans, no cheerful old ladies smiling.

I climbed some 3,000ft: no let up, no down bits to kid you that you'd already been at the top without noticing it. Every time I turned a bend, the road rose above me: and sometimes a big lorry loaded with straw, high above me, indicated something even worse, a hairpin bend!

It went on for ever: six hours of climb!

No encouraging signs saying '5 km to the Col de Ibañeta'.

True, there were kilometre markers: I worked out that it took 1,400 paces between markers (well, be fair, I didn't have much else to occupy me). Sometimes 1,380, sometimes 1,450: it was all tremendously exhilarating and I could feel my heart pounding as I neared each marker (you don't **really** believe that, do you?)

A friendly (well, he was quite surly, actually) householder, who told me that it was 3 km to the top, filled my water bottle for me.

After 2 km, I asked someone else: about 2 km!

Surly householder turned out to be right.

At the top, I'd expected some sort of celebration: but there was just a sign saying 'Col de Ibañeta 1080m', and a church and a cross.

No ice cream van, no burger bar: and lots of bored looking people in their cars, eager to spend their money on fattening, high calory food loaded up with super saturated fat, and nothing to spend it on!

What an opening for an entrepreneurial Spaniard!

Then it was down a winding track through the woods to the imposing monastery of Roncesvalles.

The other pilgrims from St Jean were already there. They'd come over the top, grinding out the hard miles: now they were lolling on the grass beneath the cedars, waiting for the Refuge to open, and I could feel their eyes silently censuring me for having taken the road rather than the high road.

They didn't know how I always lost my way, though: if I'd followed the Route Napoleon, like them, my bleached bones would probably still be out there now. Four o'clock, signing in: just like the Labour Exchange, long tables with chairs and a pile of forms which we completed and took over with our Pilgrim Passport for inspection by the Headmaster.

The single dormitory, again manned by volunteers, held 100 or more in two tiered bunks beneath the high vaulted roof. You took your shoes off at the door: **why** had I left my sandals at home to save weight? Toilets and washrooms were downstairs: they were soon swimming sociably in water, and I was soon paddling about gloomily in my bare feet.

I'd been allocated an upper bunk: I tested it out and went back to swap it for a lower bunk on the grounds of age. Actually, I was worried (having slept close to the ground for so many years) that if I got up in the night I might plummet to the ground in my semi-sleep and wake the other pilgrims with my stifled moans (I realised that we were not supposed to waken the others until 06.00) as I staunched the blood and tried to put any broken bones in traction until dawn.

Dieter was in the next bunk, bleeding feet propped up on the rail at the foot of his bunk, and his immense white teeth shining like luminous tombstones in the gloom and accentuated by the frame of his ragged black beard and moustache.

I was pleased to see that he'd taken off his tattered straw hat. He wasn't eating. Two Japanese were debating the merits of Christianity.

We drifted off to the Restaurant to have a Pilgrim Meal: it's generally composed of the dishes that the more discerning locals might not like, such as potato soup, spaghetti in tomato sauce, trout (well, they might like that, actually … oh, OK, the argument isn't always valid), yoghourt (straight from it's dinky plastic carton, rip the top off yourself), a bottle of wine, and bread: and the

The dormitory at Roncesvalles

conversation sparkled between our quartet of myself, two Basque-speaking Basques and a Japanese.

Ten o'clock, lights out: I'd filled and bounced down my Camelback so that it slowly leaked overnight into the waterproof lower compartment of my rucksack, and stuffed my bocadillo (baguette to you) filled with smelly cheese down the bungy cords on the back.

Day 2
Roncesvalles to Zubiri
22.5 km   734 km to go

The five o'clock shuffle began at – well, at about five o'clock, actually, as dark shapes began to shuffle about. The lights were actually **switched on** at six, just like Blackpool; in most

Refuges, the lights are never switched on at all for fear of upsetting somebody sleeping in.

Once, at seven o'clock, somebody actually shouted 'Silence!' from his bunk because pilgrims were talking too loudly in the still darkened room: but I'm glad to say that they all burst into spontaneous laughter.

By six, the dormitory was half empty. Shoes were still piled by the door: but I'd spirited mine away, wrapped in my towel, the previous evening and now smuggled them down to the ablutions because I really didn't like paddling about in my bare feet around the urinals. Call me over sensitive, if you like: and OK, I know that I shouldn't have left my sandals at home to reduce the weight.

Dieter had decided to rest his feet again, and prop them up against the Refuge wall during daylight hours.

I gnawed half my baguette on the bench opposite the refuge, hoisted up my rucksack, and set off. I would have set off in entirely the opposite direction if the Hospitalero at the door hadn't shouted the Spanish equivalent of 'Oy! (No, not 'hoy!', that's Spanish for 'today'): perhaps 'Hey! You're going the wrong way!'

I didn't actually **lose** my way for about a kilometre: and that was because I'd been labouring under the delusion that the direction the scallop shell waymarkers pointed, indicated the way to go.

If you think that way longterm, you've got no future on the Camino!

I went half a kilometre down a steadily narrowing track before I retraced my steps, and reappeared behind a Spanish girl carrying a busload of cellulite attached to the back of her legs.

She soon disappeared into the bushes way ahead (she'd left me miles behind!), I imagined to obey a call of nature, but reappeared carrying half a tree which she proceeded to use as a staff.

Three pilgrims who had apparently camped overnight in the graveyard outside a church were washing under the fountain in the corner before tucking into a hearty breakfast laid out on what appeared to be a gravestone.

I stopped at the Café/Bar in Espinal, like most of the other pilgrims from Roncesvalles: café grande con leche (and I **hate** coffee at home!) and 'dos tostes con dulce' (toast and jam): see, I take to Spanish like a drunk to water!

The remains of my foil wrapped baguette were still festering amongst the bungies, the cheese slowly oozing to the bottom.

The day got steadily hotter as I clawed my way up the Alto de Erro, trekking poles working overtime. I enjoyed a few kilometres through the woodland on a leafy track along the ridge before descending to Zubiri. The guidebook directions 'Continue downhill … follow the track as it gradually loses height' failed to express the sheer horror of it all to someone who'd served their apprenticeship on the cosy South Downs. I lost my way six times in all during the day: although two were, admittedly, my own fault.

Kilometre after kilometre of vertical ridges, interspersed with slippery boulders, big potholes and the occasional spiky crag (I dread to think what it would be like in a rainy winter), with the final challenge a huge shiny boulder over which you had to scramble at the side of the track masking a tiny yellow waymark arrow: and I FOUND IT!

Clambered round it, then down the final rocky track to Zubiri. I was about to lose my way again: but I said irritatedly 'Yes, I **know'** to the pilgrims who were bypassing the town and who I was about to follow before they indicated the track for me to follow. I crossed the bridge, the 'Puente de la Rabia'.

This must have been incredibly useful before medical science reached it's present heights of sophistication because, so the story goes, any animal that crossed it three times was cured of rabies. Much cheaper than a course of injections, as well. I was soon lost amidst the multi-story blocks of flats.

A lady out for a walk with the children guided me to the Refuge: a former school with a debris strewn shady school yard outside.

Now, don't think that I spend all my time complaining: but (according to the pilgrim operating the tea bar on the way down from the Alto de Perdon later), the Refuge at Zubiri is regarded as 'the pits' whenever pilgrims gather to reminisce.

And let me tell you, it certainly lives up to it's reputation!

As an innocent, even a virgin, pilgrim, I'd thought that arriving by 2 o'clock would give me lots of bunks from which to choose.

But a delighted Unchristian Theoretically Christian Spanish Lady informed me that the dormitory was 'Completo!': full, to you and me.

The previous arrival had grabbed the last bunk. 'Where is the next Refuge?' 'Five kilometres' she smiled, pointing up the road towards Larrasoaña.

'Could I sleep on the floor?'

No, said the Unchristian Theoretically Christian Spanish Lady, 'You can't!'

But a young Canadian, Benoit from Montreal, who was trying to learn English and had just spent seven months wandering round India seeking spiritual enlightenment, poked his head over the side of his bunk and told me that I could put my sleeping mat down in the gymnasium: and together with a young Spaniard from Barcelona, who'd spent most of his last three summers working in Brighton, I went down the yard to the cavernous gymnasium.

Brighton Boy spoke superb English: even so, his opening gambit, 'How is the West Pier?' took me slightly aback.

I still based myself in the dormitory (mainly because there was a table and chair) waiting for the Hospitalero: did my washing, draped it over the line to dry. There were ample showers: five, but three had no nozzle on the end of the pipe so you just got an invigorating jet of cold water, and none had a curtain so the floor was soon submerged. Two toilets sort of worked, although the doors didn't really close: no paper, of course. So, lesson one for pilgrims: whenever you visit a bar or restaurant either collect a handful of napkins, or raid the toilets (Servicios) for a good helping of the necessary. I soon had a pocketful of frayed toilet paper.

The Hospitalero appeared at 4pm, apparently happy that the pilgrims had taken over the empty building and sorted themselves out. She was a well upholstered lady beneath a mass of black curls which were fighting a losing battle with a bottle of red dye.

'Had she any old mattresses stored?' I wondered, smiling seductively as I handed over my reduced rate €2 for the night's rent.

Oh yes, and we went to the lock-up behind the neighbouring bar.

I selected one with a ragged cover for myself: Brighton Boy had to make do with a slab of foam but hey!, I reckoned it was better than nothing.

I strolled up the road for a kilometre to the café/bar and bought a Coca Cola. €1.80! I still had my craving for coke, so I sat and thought, crossed the road to the garage opposite, bought a bigger bottle for about half the price, topped up my glass, and went back into the bar to watch the Tour de France.

Back to the gymnasium and a stroll round the bars, looking for food. None. So, back up the road to the café for a Pilgrim Meal which this time really **was** what the locals didn't fancy.

The spaghetti, the waiter told me in fluent American, didn't have much tomato sauce so that I would appreciate the flavour: whilst the lumps of tuna had been home prepared, not tipped out of a tin.

I complimented him on his English.

He looked at me strangely. 'I'm from Brooklyn' he said, working in the 'folks' restaurant for the summer. I went to the Servicios and replenished my paper supply. Back at the Refuge, nobody appeared worried by the lack of paper. Benoit, who had achieved the apparently impossible by wandering round India without a stomach upset, informed me that out there he just used water.

I didn't pursue the subject: just kept a sharp eye on the washbasins whenever he was around.

The pilgrim overflow was spread thinly round the gym, which turned out to be a Pelota court. As we settled down to sleep (after all, it **was** 9.30!), an enormous electrical storm broke out. Lightning lit up the giant gym, rain lashed down on the high corrugated roof, thunder echoed round the walls. We lay petrified.

Benoit informed me next day that, in their insulated dormitory, they'd heard a bit of rain: but this, mercifully, had been drowned by the rumble of half a dozen competing snorers.

Sleep came quickly: I was woken equally quickly.

Brighton Boy was shaking my shoulder. It was 10.27.

He might have been stressed out, but at least he didn't forget his manners.

'Excuse me, the mattress you got for me is full of bed bugs'.

He flourished his blood pimpled forearms in confirmation.

We kicked our mattresses into a corner and laid down our sleeping mats.

The bed bugs didn't appear to have cross infected **my** mattress.

Brighton Boy was on his way to Pamplona to visit his aunt and uncle: I guess that he would be the source of any bed bug epidemic that might later sweep the area.

We didn't meet again.

2

Dieter, Renata – and Me

Day 3
Zubiri to Trinidad de Arre
16 km   711.5 km to go

The whirlwind of eager pilgrims swept through the Refuge shortly after five: I waited for an hour and swam into the washrooms and toilets, packed in a leisurely way, strapped my new baguette (will I ever learn?) to my rucksack bungies, and sauntered off into the still refreshing early morning.

I strolled gently round the magnesite works (what is magnesite?) on the way to Larrasoaña.

I caught up with a worried looking Lady French Teacher and her group of four curvaceous students.

'Was there a restaurant in Larrasoaña?'

'No: had I had anything to eat?'

I shook my head, trying to convey the idea that, although hungry, I would carry on bravely until I collapsed.

They gave me two cereal bars and tried to persuade me to follow them up the hill.

I carried on into town, found a restaurant for my café con leche 'fix', ate a cereal bar and half my rubbery baguette (which, now I was firmly in Spain, had become a bocadillo), and bought a natty straw hat for €4.5.

I rested my sore feet: only 16 km to Trinidad de Arre, only half a mile down the road from Villava, the birthplace and family home of Miguel Indurain.

Don't know who Miguel Indurain is? It's like asking an Englishman, who's David Beckham?

Who's **he**? Well, he's the former Manchester United and now Real Madrid player, and friend of Alex Ferguson.

Oh, you knew that already! Indurain? He rides a bicycle for a living: won the Tour de France five times, I think.

Suddenly, I realised that there were forty people ahead of me: and to my crazed mind, they represented competition for the thirty or so bunks in the Refuge. I didn't want to sleep on the floor again!

I passed about twenty of them at a lay-by, after persuading one of them to photograph me amongst their group (Oh, just a few friends that I met along the Camino!), then strode on up the dusty hillside track. Lots of them passed me again: but I leapfrogged them as they stopped for water, then shot down hill to Trinidad de Arre, constantly looking over my shoulder to see if the chasing pack was closing.

It's amazing what a night on a concrete floor will do for a Slow Walker!

I reached the Refuge, just uphill from the Basilica on the far side of the bridge, by midday: only 695.5 km to go! Wow, I was almost **there**!

Pilgrims had to 'clock in' at the church office: I was just in time to join a group of pilgrims for a guided tour of the church, with it's wonderful paintings, by the priest whose enthusiasm and devotion was an object lesson.

We stood in our rucksacks, still wearing our hats and holding

Pilgrims taking on water

our trekking poles, and sweating profusely, throughout the tour. We had our Credencials (Pilgrim Passports) stamped: I was still basking in the notion that I had won the last place in the Refuge, and thinking how well my charge down hill ahead of the chasing peloton had paid off.

The Priest let me and a couple of wizened Spanish ladies leave our rucksacks and poles in his office, because the dormitory didn't open until 14.00.

I wandered off to 'do the town'. Nice park: loved the Police Station, real modern architecture. I was back ten minutes later.

The Hospitalero was somewhat annoyed that my Credencial had been stamped upside down. I was **first back** (wow!) and he took me round the back to the superb, top of the range, Refuge.

I'd be happy with it for a home, particularly if I was expecting lots of guests eager to sleep on shelves, with nowhere to put their clothes and not too bothered about people peeking.

Sumptuous lounge, dining room, lots of books, clean showers

and toilets (unfortunately, open plan so that the full resonance of the occupants echoed round the building): great kitchen well stocked with pilgrim leftovers, from potatoes to tins of mussels and stale Spanish Mr Kipling cakes.

It was close to Paradise: and in this forty-plus bedded Refuge, there was only myself and the two wizened Spanish ladies.

One I looked at rather sharply: I think that she was the Unchristian Theoretically Christian Spanish Lady from Zubiri, but I wasn't too sure.

I decided to test my bunk by lying on it, and drifted off to sleep. By 4.30, there were eight occupants including two English who had made it from St Jean.

One, a strikingly tall Hugh Laurie look-alike, was an ex-army officer and opted for a top bunk. I guess his army training had conditioned him to seek an unobstructed field of vision so that he couldn't be taken by surprise.

His keen eyes narrowed as they swept the dormitory, before he allowed himself to relax.

His companion, older but still in the army, had the world weary cynical gaze of a shrivelled Somerset Maugham. He was obviously more fatalistic, and opted for a bottom bunk and a quick unconditional kip.

Benoit was there, with the surprised look of somebody who had got somewhere by accident: so was Renata, an Austrian clairvoyant, who had absolutely no experience of walking but had been told in a vision at Easter that she must walk the Camino.

Myself, Hugh and Somerset went to look for a pilgrim meal. Somerset spoke fluent Spanish, so all Hugh and I (Wow! That would be a good name for a TV series: must remember it just in case…) had to do was nod and say 'Yeah, me too', in an aristocratic laid-back way.

Bottle of wine, early bread (early bread is bread that rose early and aged swiftly) and guess what? Spaghetti in tomato sauce followed by the standby of the English abroad, chips, two fried eggs and spicy chorizo sausages (better than bland Walls pork chipolata!) splattered with ketchup, and a tub of bicolored ice cream (yes, a tub **each,** not between us!)

We were in danger of eating too well.

It was all we could do to stagger back to the Refuge and bed by 10.00.

Still only eight there.

Where was the chasing peloton that had been baying at my heels? Gone on to Pamplona, I guess, now that the Running with the Bulls week had passed and freed up the accommodation.

I sighed, and went to sleep.

Day 4
Trinidad de Arre to Cizur Menor
7.5 km   695.5 km to go

Hugh and Somerset sprang into action early, eager for another 50 km: Benoit, Renata and myself took a more leisurely approach as we ransacked the kitchen.

Benoit cut up potatoes and onions: Renata fried them up: and I ate them.

Renata and myself were soon on our way to Pamplona Post Office to post home all the items that we hadn't thought we could do without when we started.

Benoit sauntered off ahead, loosely in touch with us as we tried to navigate with our Guide Book. I soon gave up and resorted to saying to kindly looking passers-by 'Correos (Post Office), por favor?' and raising a quizzical eyebrow.

This was fairly frequent, because their rapid fire reply put enormous strain on my ten word Spanish vocabulary and I could only take one idea on board at a time (like, first left, second right). Mime was better.

Sadly, Renata didn't want to make a detour to pay homage to Miguel Indurain.

What a talking point this would have been (accompanied by a fuzzy photograph, maybe even a slide!) when I got home.

You know, 'This is where Miguel Indurain was brought up'.

'Oh yes? Very interesting' (Thinks: who's Miguel Indurain?)

Long pause: then perhaps, 'This is a picture of Pamplona Post Office'

'Ah yes, that looks nice: good gracious, is that the time, I must be going'.

They were so used to pilgrims sending back unwanted baggage at Pamplona Post Office that the man behind the counter didn't even smile as he took the regular box down from the shelf.

Binoculars, a fleece (in case it gets cold at night, I'd thought: I wasn't aware, then, that in Spain they close windows and shutters at night in the Refuges to build up a really good fug and they're not happy until the temperature has soared beyond 100ºF and everybody has stripped off every vestige of clothing and lies sweating on top of their sleeping bag), plug transformer, third pair of trousers, third shirt…, it weighed 3 kg and cost almost £20.00, but boy! was it worthwhile!

A German pilgrim sent home 12 kg: goodness knows what **he** had brought, but he must have floated out of the Post Office afterwards.

I'd already donated my cutlery to the kitchen at Trinidad de Arre, because it was in danger of puncturing my Camelback water container which was already leaking everywhere and providing a trickle of cool water down my back that was dribbling off the bottom of my shorts.

We celebrated with a coffee: it was obviously a popular café/bar in the centre of Pamplona, judging by the thick carpet of cigarette ends and paper piled up on the floor against the counter.

I looked round furtively, and filled my pocket with Pilgrims Insurance from the paper napkin dispenser on the table.

We strolled through the busy streets, and after a stretch through the wooded grounds of the University of Navarre followed by a large and imaginative road building complex, hit the sunbaked hard shoulder and the long drag up to Cizur Menor.

The Knights of St John of Malta hadn't got round to opening their Refuge yet, so we plodded on for a few hundred yards to a wonderful, sheltered 'private' Refuge with a great welcome: only 7.5 km for the day, but it felt like 27.5 km as I limped gingerly on my battered feet into the shaded sixteen bed bungalow.

I followed the Second Rule for pilgrims: wash your clothes **first**, yourself **second**, when you reach a Refuge otherwise there'll be no room left on the line.

I stretched my clothes out on the drying frames in the building site at the back, next to the concrete mixer: dust, Alsatians and builders everywhere and yet it all felt very safe.

I sat beneath the grape laden vines outside the bungalow to browse through my weighty collection of guide books, along with all the other pilgrims planning their next day's route. Most pilgrims were satisfied with one guide book: I'd brought **three**, just to be on the safe side.

My blood ran cold when I glanced at the *Pilgrim Guide to Spain*: still 702 km to go! Yesterday, according to Alison Raju, only 695.5 km remained. Had I, after a hard day, somehow lost 7.5 km? The first two guides only agreed distances at Santiago (zero): the third didn't like to venture an opinion, but it was entertaining reading.

I decided to stick with Alison for distance: you'd get there quicker with her!

Moral: read the right guide book, otherwise you'll only upset yourself unnecessarily!

Pilgrim meal: you don't even need to ask what we ate! Well, surprise, surprise: we had macaroni, not spaghetti, but of course smothered in the obligatory tomato sauce.

I still laboured under the delusion that a bocadillo on my back would stave off starvation. Slight problem with this one, though: when the bloke behind the bar asked what filling I wanted for my breakfast tempter, I shrugged and gestured towards a chap further down the bar who was savaging a bocadillo with obvious enjoyment.

I ended up with hot omelette filling, which carried on simmering in it's kitchen foil wrapping and by morning looked, felt and tasted like playdough.

I couldn't face it for breakfast next morning, so saved it for an early lunch: it didn't appeal then, either, but I forced half of it down in desperation.

Day 5
Cizur Menor to Puente la Reina
21 km   688 km to go

Renata and I started late: it took her half an hour to tape up her toes.

We immediately lost our way: trouble is, our friendly guide book said 'Pass *frontón* on right', and it was only when we were well down the wrong road looking for a *'frontón'* (whatever that might be) that we realised it probably meant the pelota court which was being passed by a long line of pilgrims way back up the hill.

Now, the previous evening the lady at the Refuge had kindly offered to transport our baggage on to Puente la Reina: FREE!

What a generous gesture!

Yes, she said, the new Refuge there is just through the town. 600m along the main street, and it's just up on the right. Well, it is: but 'just up on the right' meant a half kilometre climb of awesome steepness, especially after 20+ km and eleven hours on the Camino.

But it's a great sales gimmick: we **had** to go there to get our kit back!

Anyway, we hadn't settled in to 'the first ten days are the worst' groove yet: and we'd started off much to late at 7.00. It seems great to have a lie-in, watching Renata taping her toes: but we'd missed an hour of cool walking.

We slogged up the hill to the bar at Zaregui: who should be there but Dieter, tombstones flashing menacingly, feet spectacularly restored.

Renata and myself left first: a 5 km trudge up the scrub covered hillside to the top of the Alto de Perdón high on the ridge and flanked on either side by forty modern windmills garnering power for Pamplona.

'Some people say that it spoils the environment' observed a Spaniard: 'but I think that it makes a wonderful modern artistic statement.'

I kept quiet: it would certainly have roused Don Quixote, and it terrified me. But in a strange way, I could see what he meant.

On the summit was a monument and an enormous linear iron cut-out sculpture depicting pilgrims on foot and horseback, plus two donkeys and a dog. The inscription read '*donde se cruza el camino del viento con ci de las estrellas*' ('where the path of the wind crosses that of the stars'), plus on a more practical note a reference to the part played by the Eolic Wind Power Company

Lining up with the other pilgrims on the Alto de Perdón

and the Electricity Board of Navarre, which brought it all nicely down to earth. There's a legend about it all, as well: but as it's a bit long winded (long **winded**! Get it? Oh well, never mind), it's best to look it up elsewhere if you're **really** interested.

On a more prosaic note, pilgrims who could go no further were entitled to pardon from half their sins (which half, I don't know).

We all posed for the obligatory photographs on the summit, taking our place in the pilgrim line-up beside the donkeys.

Maggie (a Canadian of Venezuelan extraction) and her Dutch companion clicked the camera for us: but it can't have been unexpected for Maggie because she, like Renata, was a professional clairvoyant.

It must have been a bit boring for them when they walked together: I guess both of them must have known what the other was thinking, and what their reply would be, so they didn't need to talk.

We slithered down the rocky path towards Uterga: I had spent part of a sleepless night worrying about this, after the warning from Brighton Boy that it 'made the path down to Zubiri from the Alto de Erro seem like paradise'. It was, he said, the worst of the worst.

Well, BB, I've got news for you: with care, and a trekking pole, it was only about twice as bad as the worst part of the South Downs Way.

As it levelled out, I saw the roof of a caravan beside the track.

My heart leapt: a Mr Whippy van!

I legged it for a Magnum.

Well, it **was** a caravan: staffed by the Amigos de Camino (or similar), a wonderful group of people who throughout the summer (my host, the self styled St Bedford Bedouin was doing a six month stint!) meet pilgrims along the way, and provide drinks, help and support at some of the more difficult places, a sort of Spiritual Get You Home Service.

St Bedford Bedouin

Renata and myself lounged on their deckchairs and used the superb toilet facilities (al fresco, pick your own space and peek between the shrubs to see if there's anybody coming your way, with the breeze ruffling your hair, sun beating down, the soft grass caressing you gently and the warm smell of rosemary and fennel whenever you moved).

Renata wanted to visit Eunate, one of the Holy Places of Spain: an awesome octagonal church, possibly dating back to the mystical Knights Templars in the 12th century and set in isolation amidst the fields. It was a place for silent meditation.

We left the Camino and wandered down a little lane for a few kilometres to Eunate. Dieter was there, sitting in silent contemplation.

He translated from the Spanish notice board, that visitors should remove their shoes and socks and, barefoot, walk three times around the little church on the path of stones set on edge that encircled it and then, barefoot still, stand at the entrance awaiting the spiritual bidding to enter.

Dieter and Renata, despite their hideously beat up feet, managed this in double quick time. I managed one circuit in fifteen minutes still wearing my double skinned socks, moaning softly, eyes half closed as I felt my way along the wall.

I did another two circuits on the grass beyond the arches.

Renata said it didn't matter, I had at least tried. I regretted the fact that Dieter could read Spanish so well, otherwise we'd never have known.

But I still felt this sense of awe and peace when I entered.

It was now gone three o'clock: Dieter had remained at Eunate to continue meditating, and the guide book promised an easy walk along a sheltered footpath beside the road for 3 km straight into Puente la Reina.

Eunate

Well, it didn't quite work out like that.

We followed the giant yellow arrows, the *flechas*, that marked the Camino, up an awesome hill into Obanos where, Renata told me, every other year they hold a mammoth arts festival in the village square at **exactly** this time of year with 800 extras from the village and an audience of thousands.

Well, I wouldn't have thought 800 people in total lived in Obanos: more like 80, and even that would have been stretching it. I was just glad that it took place last year and next year.

I just said 'Wow! That's really interesting' in a conversation killing tone of voice, and hoped that she wouldn't expand on the subject because I was getting a bit tired. Down the hill we went to the road we'd left an hour or so before (and only about 100 metres further along): there were still 3 km to Puente la Reina.

Every half hour, Renata kept saying 'I'm sure we've come more than 3 km' and I grunted.

When we at last entered the town, she decided that she wanted to visit a church (after two hours at Eunate!); she meditated for half an hour, then we set off on the long drag through the town to get re-united with our sleeping bags.

We soon passed the other Refuge: I looked at it longingly. A kilometre to go. It was already 6 pm: 11 hours on foot in blazing sun and unexpectedly, we didn't feel tired.

Up the final hill we crawled: and there was a paradise amongst Refuges!

Palatial is the word that springs to mind and stays there.

You could see almost to Santiago one way, and had it not been for the Pyrenees, to St Jean the other. Well, that's possibly stretching it a bit: but you could certainly see the windmills beside the Alto de Perdón.

There were 64 bunks in the half full main dormitory, with enough room in the centre for an indoor tennis court: and more eight bed dormitories led off a further distant corridor.

We collected our plastic sacks from the Hospitalero, a depressed wizened chain smoking pensioner who added up things like three postcards and stamps laboriously on pieces of paper.

There was a huge washing room, with washing machine and spin dryer that nobody was skilled enough to use: I had a surreptitious twiddle at the knobs, which now seem inextricably locked. I'm sure it was like that when I started.

But there were few toilets for this magnificent building: two sit downers, two showers and one wash basin for men and I assume (I didn't check it personally) the same for women. Good job I'd stocked up on paper napkins earlier, as well.

As for the Dining Room: well, it seated at least 100, with an enormous bar that curved the entire width of the room. The Hospitalero gloomily occupied one end, beside the telephone from which I rang England. €2 lasted seemingly for ever.

The macaroni and tomato sauce opener was followed by

eggs, chips and chorizo sausage, followed by the intriguingly named 'flan'.

Jus another name for yoghourt: you peel back the lid as usual.

But the wine! I asked for a glass full, and it arrived in a pint tankard, three quarters full. It made up for it's modest origins by sheer aggression.

I slept well, surrounded by a dozen empty bunks. Renata was about a quarter of a mile away, on the other side of the room.

Day 6
Puente la Reina to Estella
23 km   667 km to go

Breakfast at 6.00am was like eating in a palace: if you were that way inclined, you could even have eaten off the floor. My fresh cheese bocadillo (will I ever learn?), bought over the bar that morning, was soon sweating inside a Sainsbury's carrier bag and squeezed into my rucksack bungies.

Sun cream on: essential, particularly in view of the fact that I was walking to raise money for sun-induced melanoma (skin cancer) research.

Bacteria were soon multiplying in their cosy cheesy pressure cooker: their breeding rate must have risen alarmingly as soon as the sun began to beat down on my back along the Camino.

Sunglasses weren't always a great help through the day, because invariably the sun was either at our backs or behind the left shoulder, although they took the edge off the constant glare: but you'd be crazy not to carry them.

As soon as the sun got high in the sky (like, 06.30!), you realised that a light, broadbrimmed breathable hat is essential: straw hats are great, or something 'cool' in the outback style, but without the corks.

Heavy hats are a no-no, though: you realise that, when the sweat begins to run in rivulets down your neck and brow.

Protect the back of your neck, as well as the crown of your head: and it's a good idea to turn up your collar or wear a light scarf. Me, I wore a teatowel tucked beneath the rear brim of my hat, decorated with tasteful views of the Derbyshire Peak District. It had done such good service in my kitchen for so many years that it was quite threadbare and cool: and after all, it reminded me of home.

Renata thought that she would leave at 8.00, after she had finished her complex toe taping.

So, not unwillingly, I set off alone after rescuing my clothes from the barbed wire fence where they'd been blown from the washing line behind the windswept Refuge.

A couple of windmills up there, and they'd have solved the electricity problem for the whole town.

I **like** walking alone. So do most pilgrims. Apart from giving us time to think, we can stop when and where we want without mentally putting ourselves in the place of our companion (Is he getting tired?): and of course, if we are caught up by another pilgrim they are going too fast for us, and if we catch up with another pilgrim, they are going too slowly!

Even the groups that I met were invariably in single file along the narrow trails, not speaking, doggedly trudging onwards: evenings at the Refuges or over a pilgrim meal were the times to swap stories, relax and reminisce.

Walking the Camino with a friend must be great: but during the day, frustration is eased if you each set your own pace. Anyway, for me it was no problem: I was by myself.

I soon met a climbing wall of red earth, summed up rather charmingly in the Guide Book as 'forking L … to a ravine and then follow it (now a FP) uphill again'.

Translated into real life speak, it meant clambering/stepping over deep gullies that ravaged the hillside for about a kilometre: but after that, it was a great walk.

I replenished my water store at the shaded fountain in the square opposite the lovely church in the beautiful mediaeval village of Cirauqui. The Camelback soon oozed water companionably down my back.

The square was littered with pilgrims, slumped against the shady walls. No bar!

What a business opportunity! Perhaps I should emigrate and start one there … no, perhaps not. Just a thought.

I had a vigorous swing in the children's playground instead to shake my brains back into place and take the weight off my feet.

I strolled gently down the hill and crossed an old bridge.

Good job I'd topped up my camelback, I thought, as I came to a second bridge.

A thousand years or so ago, Pope Calixtus had (apparently, according to dear old Aymery Picaud) warned pilgrims not to drink from this particular river, or to water their horses there, because (as he said, rather succinctly in a manner that would have been the envy of any modern ad man) 'the river brings death'.

He hammers home the message by telling how a pilgrim had noticed a couple of locals sharpening their knives by the side of the stream: and he'd asked them, as you do, if it was good drinking water for the horses.

'Yes' they said (or, probably, 'Si'): at which he watered a couple of his horses which promptly dropped dead. Must have been pretty quick acting, by the sound of it.

The locals then skinned them on the spot.

I peered over the bridge and was reassured to see lots of fish of all sizes swimming about busily: perhaps the water had been cleaned up since those days, but even so, a can of something or other seemed a wiser investment.

Hope the village fountain fed the river, as well, rather than the other way round.

You can't be too careful, after all.

Through Villatuerta: got my passport stamped (a *sello*, stamp) in the spotless entrance to a new private Refuge. It's a growing business: but at only €5, it's still largely motivated by Charity.

It was only 12.53 when I reached Estella: and already pilgrims thronged the entrance.

Got a bunk: and who should be lying on one of the staff bunks in the second floor corridor but Benoit!

He'd spent the night after we had parted at Pamplona, sleeping at Eunate.

A couple who acted as caretakers and lived in the nearby house had room for two pilgrims, free, and he had enjoyed a private service with them there in the church that night.

Now he was helping out for a couple of days at the Refuge in Estella. How could he afford to travel the world like this, I wondered. It appeared that the unworldly Benoit had majored in computers at University in Montreal and had set up a thriving IT business which was being run by a friend in his absence.

'If it goes bust', and he shrugged, 'then so what?': and he lay back on his bunk and slept a little longer.

Even then, the dormitory was pretty full. Opposite me was Julia from Gloucester and, in the top bunk, her cousin Rachel who was suffering from an unspecified illness: so the Gloucester Girls had stayed for an extra day. Couldn't help thinking; if she was ill, wouldn't it have been easier for her to have the bottom bunk? Oh well, none of my business.

The Brits were in danger of taking over the Refuge: further down were the English Roses, girl and boyfriend, who seemed in a beautiful haze, totally immersed in each other's company as they gazed into each other's eyes. Their relationship seemed so pure, so innocent: and their contentment was complete.

What, I wondered, will they be like together in twenty, or ten, or even two years: I hoped that it wasn't just the sweet innocence of youth, that first blissful love affair. I was so pleased to get a bunk that I broke my golden rule: I showered before I washed my clothes.

I still had no pegs, and the washing lines were full, but I was so intoxicated by arriving early that I went overboard with the washing. I washed my towel, my shorts, all my spare socks: and I had nowhere to hang them, and nothing to hang them up with even if I had!

A tall sun tanned French pilgrim, a caricature of Larry Grayson, polkadotted red head scarf knotted loosely behind his long black tresses, stood watching with a hand on his hip and an aloof pout as I laid my clothes on the hot paving in the back garden, beneath a colourful mural along the garden wall above the washing line.

His two little friends, The Boys, stood silently at his side, hands occasionally touching. They never did say much: but then, they didn't need to.

I sat down in the large kitchen with a cold coke for a chat with Shamak, a Polish film script writer and producer based in Berlin who spoke far better English than me.

He gave me some of his bubbling pan full of macaroni (and tomato sauce, would you guess?) and beans: I bought him a beer from the machine.

By the time we'd finished, I went out to check my washing, hopefully evaporating on the stone paving, only to discover it

Hanging out the washing at Estella

neatly bundled up in a festering heap on the washing line.

I have my suspicions.

Draped it over the line as best I could (and subtly 'borrowed' a few pegs from overpegged garments); made a mental note, MUST GET SOME PEGS OF MY OWN! But would you believe it, by 5.30 everything was dry!

Dieter arrived, tombstones flashing: a weary Renata had gone to her bunk. She does so well: no training, just obeying a calling that she had received at Easter, and she has just got up and done it. I applaud them: both are typical pilgrims in the original 'spiritual' mould.

I wandered down to the Spar supermarket and BOUGHT SOME PEGS, a block of carbolic soap for myself and some more cold water washing gel. In my innocence, I still thought that it mattered.

Soon, I used the carbolic for my clothes, pummelling them on the scrubbing board, and the washing gel for my hair. I reckoned that, if it was suitable for fine silks and soft fabrics, it would be alright for me.

HOW TO CROSS THE ROAD IN SPAIN

I wandered round the town, dicing with death on the pedestrian crossings. So I'll tell you how they work: no, I don't think it's written in the Spanish Highway Code.

Firstly, there appears to be a marker line in the middle of the road: if you haven't reached this, then traffic coming in the opposite direction doesn't stop anyway. You can't even begin to approach this central marker unless there is absolutely **nothing** coming on your side: if you step off the pavement in front of a car, you're fair game.

Remember, you're pretty isolated standing in the centre of a Spanish road: crossing the road in Spain is character forming.

Secondly, standing in the centre of the road and twitching nervously, wait until a car coming in the opposite direction is quite a long way off before you put a foot over the line into **his** sector.

If you are tentative, they won't stop anyway: but if you appear confident, drivers carry on with foot hovering over brake pedal to see which of you will crack first.

Actually, they've been looking at you all along, to see if you show signs of real commitment: and if you make a sudden lunge, they'll shudder to a stop pretending they'd meant to stop all along.

So, if you can keep your resolve, the oncoming car will stop!

If you can't, you don't deserve to cross the road anyway.

Best thing, though, is to mingle with a group of nuns: it's generally regarded as bad luck to knock down a nun.

But there aren't even many **individual** nuns around in Estella, let alone a group of them.

So if you can't tag onto a nun, it's best to wait until you can see absolutely **nothing** coming in either direction: and even then, you'd better nip across pretty smartish because cars tend to arrive at speed just when you're least expecting them.

Oh yes, thirdly, Good Luck.

No wonder, if you live in a town, you reside on the same side of the street as the shops that you use most frequently.

MEANWHILE, BACK AT THE REFUGE

The temperature was still 29°C (84°F in old currency) at 6.22pm.

There were no pilgrim's meals to be had in any of the town's 25 restaurants: so I HAD TO COOK MY OWN!

I ended up with a huge plate of pasta and tinned tomato. Couldn't finish it: even Shamak rejected it.

The only excitement was when Renata's red trousers, hanging over the balcony to dry, blew over next door: and she couldn't get them back, because the lady in the next house didn't answer the door. It turned out that she'd died.

A young German scaled the wall and threw the trousers back. They landed on the roof and, with colleagues, he had to mount a further rescue operation using a clothes prop whilst balanced on the balcony rail.

Ah well, it's all part of the exciting life of the Camino!

I had a long involved discussion about LIFE with a Dutch biologist, packed my bag, and went to bed squashed tightly on half of what was virtually a double bed with a naked Frenchman, who had discarded his sleeping bag for the night, and who kept rolling ominously towards me.

Day 7
Estella to Los Arcos
20 km   644 km to go

Wow! They even served breakfast from 05.30, €3.5 for as much as you could eat! Sadly, it wasn't bacon and eggs: toast and biscuits with cheese spread or jam.

I was waiting for a seat when at 06.00 there was a loud explosion followed by the Basque Choir and associated musicians striking up in the street outside the Refuge before they walked to the church with those pilgrims who wished in procession behind.

It was July 25th, the feast of St James.

I stood and listened, even forgoing my breakfast for an hour: the music had a raw charm like so much ethnic music (no, I'm not being condescending, I really loved it!)

By the time I'd got sorted, even Dieter and Renata were ahead of me: and at 6.45 it was already hot. Turned out the explosion was nothing to do with the band, but the tourist office being blown up by a group of extremists.

Too late now to drop in and get a walking tour leaflet, as the Guide Book suggested.

We had to be re-routed round town, on the hill route.

Up and up I toiled, trailing three ladies without rucksacks (one was the Unchristian Theoretically Christian Spanish Lady from Zubiri) and one with a large carrier bag.

I asked her if she'd drawn the short straw for the day. She smiled nervously: but as she only spoke Spanish it was all wasted on her. It turned out that a camp follower had carried the rucksacks on in his car: something that was more and more common.

But we soon zipped downhill to the Monastery of Irache,

Even I can't lose my way here!

lured by the promise of a free drink.

A local bodega sponsored a twin jet fountain: one jet dispensing fresh mountain water, the other red wine (with the wish that pilgrims wouldn't abuse this!).

Well, either the pilgrims (or the locals? Surely not!) had already abused it, or the duty Wine Dispenser hadn't turned it on yet that morning. You could smell the wine, you could see traces in the bowl, but the jet was dry.

It turned out that the wine didn't start flowing until 10.30: the Guide Book rather primly suggested that 'A little discretion is advised on hot afternoons'.

Good marketing, this late opening. By that time, all the poor thirsty pilgrims with nil purchasing power are long gone: whilst the coach loads of tourists, all busting to replenish their cellars, were arriving for free samples.

The Monastery looked great, but that was closed as well: Renata and Dieter were disappointed about this, they told me when I caught them up at the next village (Azqueta) where we all trooped in to the house of Pablito Sanz to augment our passports with a *sello*, because they'd hoped to get in an early church to start the day off on a good footing. They should have consulted **their** Guide Book as well: Monastery opening hours 1000 to 1400, and every afternoon except Tuesday (Why? Early closing day in Irache perhaps?), were once more geared up for tourists rather than pilgrims. Oh yes, it's closed all day Monday as well in case you're planning a visit.

Pablito Sanz is a smiley grey bearded man, another of the 'characters' of the Camino, famous for giving pilgrims the long hazel staffs which they can often be seen carrying, which must keep him fully occupied even if only 1% of the 25,000 pilgrims each year take advantage of his kindness.

He also maintains a nice toilet: I carried a wad of his paper around as my insurance policy for days.

I filled up my Camelback at the village fountain: good job, because a hot, flat 12 km lay ahead. No houses, just the odd stack of straw bales, as I walked along the white ribbon of road winding into the distance between the shaven wheat fields that filled this deep yellow bowl, the symmetry broken only by odd rounded hills studded with conifers, and framed by a rim of distant mountains beneath a deep blue sky.

It was still only just after midday when I reached the Refuge in Los Arcos.

Los Arcos had been an important town in bygone days: and although it was now reduced to a large bustling village, it boasted a wonderful church, just across the square from the new gleaming white Refuge which charged only €3.

It was a 'family business' Refuge, with Albert and Paola's quarters behind the desk around which pilgrims were clustering. English speaking Paola told me, when I thanked her for her help,

'It is a pleasure: we are here to serve'.

Even the notices were bilingual: 'If water falls down, use the mop. Please'.

2.30, Renata arrived: 4.30, Dieter arrived.

How had I passed them? Dieter flashed his tombstones and remarked 'I sleeped in the fields'.

I collapsed onto a (lower) bunk in a dark shady corner of the 30+ bedded dormitory: Larry Grayson, on the next bunk once again, pouted in greeting when he saw me and tossed his sleek hair petulantly. The Boys were just across the room and stared blankly. I just hoped that they weren't jealous. Their fingers sought each other for mutual support.

The Gloucester Girls were tucked away in a distant corner.

Would you believe it, there was a mangle in the yard beside the sink, just like my mother used to wring out the clothes fifty (oh, alright, sixty) years ago outside the washhouse. A young (well, 30+ year old) pilgrim rhapsodised about this wonderful machine that squeezed out the water so that there was no need to wrap your towel round the taps and twist.

I was glad that he didn't immediately rush off to file a patent: it would be rather like Bill Gates re-inventing the wheel.

I proudly hung up my clothes with my new bright green pegs: the purple ones in the pack seemed a little gloomy and, ever generous, I tried to give them away to needy pilgrims.

Good job my generosity was spurned: most of the green ones had been pinched a week later, and I was glad of the purple.

Now for a shower.

Nothing's simple where Refuge washrooms are concerned.

The shower and the toilet were, for some strange reason, integral.

You entered the toilet and locked the door, then entered the shower through the open doorway in the facing wall.

So you monopolised both for the sake of a shower, whilst desperate pilgrims pounded on the door.

I felt really bad about this (I'm all heart, really) and as soon as I was half dry, I dashed out with my cake of cheap carbolic and finished drying in the yard.

As the shower had no curtain or door, the toilet floor was soon swimming with water: it's all geared up to maximise the spread of verruca and athlete's feet.

Someone could do a really boring Ph. D. thesis, comparing the verruca and athlete's foot status of a group of pilgrims at, say, Roncesvalles and their status at Santiago... no, I'm getting carried away again. I just lack this critical faculty or the ability to set out such experiments but, heck, you know what I mean. Oh, just forget it!

Anyway, it's good here: cans of Coke €0.65 from the machine compared with €1.00 at Estella.

I nipped into town to buy my breakfast: everywhere was shut, it was the Feast Day of St James. I found a *panaderia* (bread shop) which was still getting rid of the morning surplus, and battled with needy pilgrims for a stale roll.

No Pilgrim Meals anywhere: all the café/bars were shut.

There was to be a service in the church.

But to our delight, Albert (or Paola? One or the other, anyway) told us that this would be followed by **a free meal for Pilgrims in the Refuge yard**.

Guess what I think it will be.

Well, you're wrong!

It was a typical Basque meal, potato and meat soup, with red wine, followed by melon and watermelon, and biscuits: and it was FREE! It wasn't even conditional on going to the church service that preceded it, and collecting a voucher.

As Dieter said, 'Not bad for €3'.

Now, I'm not a Catholic: but the Mass that preceded the meal was incredibly powerful. Almost every pilgrim attended.

The church of Santa Maria was totally impressive: the wall behind the altar was intricately carved and decked in gold, from floor to high roof, as were the side chapels and walls, whilst the ceiling and the cupola were painted with biblical scenes. Every inch of the huge church had been decorated with loving care, testimony to the power of the Church and it's complete integration with everyday life in Spain from mediaeval times until the present day: and of course, these wonderful churches, monasteries, refuges and associated villages and hamlets had evolved as the Pilgrim Support Service along the Camino, which had been an integral part of life in this northern part of Spain for a thousand years.

It was a very humbling experience.

I looked up at the vaulted roof: I could see deep cracks extending across the cupola.

I was glad that I wasn't sitting in the centre of the church.

The pilgrims each received a blessing: then we visited the central rose garden amidst the cloisters (no black spot on the roses!)

Renata was in tears: but she took my photograph for me.

Outside the church, I met the English Roses. They were staying at the private Refuge up the road: €6.5 and no free meal!

All the rest of us went back to eat, sitting sociably beside the long tables, with the food cooked in a huge cauldron in the shed and served up by the Amigos de Camino. It had been a super day.

3

Rioja: Red Wine and Carnival

Day 8 July 26th

Los Arcos to Logroño

26 km   624 km to go

Now, I know the lights don't go on until 06.00: but the tactical battle starts an hour or so earlier.

Surreptitious stirrings: the odd muffled alarm clock.

Shadowy figures whispering to each other: the rustle of rucksacks being clumsily stuffed, pilgrims eager to get away by first light, well before 0600 in mid-summer.

But the **real** tactical battle is concerned with unhampered use of the toilets.

I looked at my watch every two minutes: when was the latest possible time to break cover, to grab the facilities ahead of the queue, quick brush of the teeth (don't take your towel, you need to keep it dry for the day. That's why you never have a shower in the morning: for sensible pilgrims, early afternoon on the day of arrival is the last possible shower time. After that, you just wipe your hands on your shorts).

Rucksack packed the previous night: just keep the space open for the sleeping bag.

But if you are ready **too** early, it's too dark to see: and it's always best not to be first pilgrim away, or you have no fall guy to follow. You could see early packers lurking in a dark corner of the yard, giving the first group away ten seconds start and then keeping near enough to hear their muffled imprecations as they tripped over kerbs or potholes and dropped their torch, but **far** enough away not to be included in any decision making when they got lost.

I tell you, it's an art that you have to learn: and I was still in the first ten days of a steep learning curve.

05.20? Too early: but I surreptitiously slipped on my socks, shoes and shorts, a difficult trick lying on your back on a constricted bunk and pretending that you're just having an early morning scratch, and trying not to send out alarm signals to all the other pilgrims who are also looking for just the right moment to strike.

05.26? Ideal: got it!

For six minutes, I'd been getting this same tingling that I used to get waiting for the starting gun for a race: muscles tightening, breathing getting quicker, a tense feeling as the adrenalin flooded my system.

Then, pow! This was the moment to strike! (Over the top – what, me? Never!)

I sprang from my bunk, sidestepping rucksacks and the occasional somnolent pilgrim.

First in: frantic search for toilet with paper. No luck: had to revert to my stash of restaurant napkins. Quick dash for washbasin, before the chorus of vigorous tooth brushing began. Sometimes, participants would wander round the dormitory, packing with one hand and brushing with the other: those with battery powered brushes could keep going for ages as they assaulted their bleeding gums.

05.30? Too late: the mass shadowy rising was in full swing, toilets were under pressure.

05.40 Ready to leave: so were Renata (unusually) and Dieter.

Where did Renata and Dieter go? Missed them: ah, away alone as I prefer, climbing up the rough road behind groups of shadowy pilgrims to the small hilltop village of Sansol and through Torres del Río.

The next few kilometres were challenging! Steep rises and falls, digging my way up and down hill with my trusty trekking poles, descending the Barranco Mataburros (the Donkey Killing Ditch. Why? Don't know: don't even ask!). Sweat poured off me as the sun rose: I felt in a daze. It seemed a long way to Viana, with it's cool paved streets and tables overflowing from bars onto the wide pavements, customers lounging in their seats watching the world go by.

I got a *sello* at both the Tourist Office and the church, where a stone in front of the main door (his tomb is now beneath the road, we are told) commemorates Cesare Borgia, a son of a 17th century Pope, who had been assassinated nearby.

Son, did I say?

The church at Viana with the grave of Cesare Borgia

Ah well, as Dieter said philosophically later, these things happen! I was soon in La Rioja: visions of rough red wine swam before my eyes, overpriced at €1 a bottle but worth it, believe me!

It was a long road drag into Logroño.

Logroño, through which I, my wife and the three boys used to drive in our Commer Dormobile in the old days thirty five years ago on the way to the magical Sierra de Cazorla in south east central Spain to collect plant specimens for Kew Gardens and the British Museum, had been a charming old city.

But the outskirts are now clogged with heavy industry, whilst the large city centre has become increasingly sophisticated. It's been rapidly overtaken by 'progress' to become a bustling city of 120,000 people.

Cross the bridge over the Ebro, turn right up a sheltered street: and there's the Refuge, up a little alley on the left!

Thankfully, it's in the 'old quarter' behind the cathedral: and you can let 'progress' pass you by.

I entered a large paved shaded courtyard, early pilgrims lolling on the universal white plastic chairs: and my aching feet began to twitch at the sight.

It was 1.39 in the afternoon: well into the heat of the day after 26 km, and a time when all good pilgrims should be sheltering somewhere cool.

Check in: second floor dormitory. Head to toe with Larry Grayson, in close proximity for the third successive night.

He pouted recognition and extended his fingers in an exaggerated gesture. The Boys were immersed in each other's company.

Broke my golden rule again: showered first, **then** did the washing. Had to push up the other washing on the drooping multi string driers to get any space.

A thought: why don't the young, fit, early arrivals get sent to the top bunks on the top floor, leaving the lower bunks on the ground floor for the old beat-up late-arriving pilgrims for whom every step further is an individual torment?

I guessed it wouldn't catch on, though: until I reached Portomarín, where my faith in human nature was vindicated! But you'll have to wait another 26 days for that!

I decided to tend to my feet, like most of the other pilgrims who were engaged in the afternoon pastime of gloomily inspecting each others feet: most weren't supple enough to examine their own, and anyway, it's nice to take part in group activities with your friends. I found it difficult, but did my best. After all, nothing puts off another pilgrim, to whom you haven't yet been introduced, more than saying 'Excuse me, could you have a look at my feet and give an honest opinion about their state of repair?'

I took off about a square inch of thick dead skin, applied a Compeed type pad, and hoped for the best.

CONCERT TIME

Would you believe it, another concert and free meal. But not until 7.30pm: time to shop for breakfast first.

The Bronzed German Cyclist, who had half his household strapped to his bike, and who had kindly swapped his bottom bunk with me as a gesture to Help the Aged, told me of a food shop not a hundred yards away.

I thought I'd find it by another route: no, I'll never learn!

I soon found myself in the main square, in front of the church: it was swathed in scaffolding and plastic sheeting. The entrance was the only visible part, the arch above split with zigzag cracks just like the cupola at Los Arcos.

Sophisticated cafés lined the square. Larry and The Boys

were there: he extended a limp wrist in my direction. The Boys ignored me again. They do it well.

The main shopping streets were wide and glitzy. My request for a *panaderia* (bread shop) or a *supermercado* (supermarket) fell on shrugging shoulders.

I suppose it was rather like asking for the nearest bakers, or Sainsburys, in Piccadilly Circus.

I spread out in wider and wider circles. After an hour, I found a *panaderia* that claimed to be open at 6pm. Five minutes to go: every five minutes after that, I rattled the shuttered door angrily. At 6.20 an elegant lady informed me that it was closed on Saturdays.

Ah! So it was Saturday, was it? I checked later: she was right.

But she directed me to a 'large, open *supermercado*'.

It was awash with Saturday afternoon Spanish apathy.

Oranges? Only by the bag full. Bananas? Gone. Bread? Only plastic bags of four soft, textureless buns. Cake? Of a sort.

I spent €4.5 on things that I didn't like, and swam in a sea of sweat back to the Refuge. It was, I noticed, 40°C at 5.50pm: 104°F in old currency.

I was told that it was 46°C in Seville (115°F): glad that we were in the cooler north.

There was a bustle of seats being put out for the Concert. The meal was apparently conditional on attendance. Even the washing had been shifted.

The sinks were in full blazing sun: the drying area was in the shade, anyway. My socks were still wet. I felt a sense of foreboding.

The Concert, by an elegant uniformed choir from Pamplona, fell in between many stools.

Surely they hadn't been forced to travel this far to find a receptive audience of foreigners, who they were to feed to ensure their attendance?

Well, perhaps they had, I decided afterwards: but only because they hadn't got the mix right.

The energetic little conductor could have enthused for Spain.

The choir was rehearsed to the nth degree: so much so, that the passion had got lost along the way. Only one lady amongst the 24 strong group bubbled with infectious enthusiasm, and looked as if she were genuinely glad to be there. Perhaps she'd missed a lot of the rehearsals.

The music was sadly one pace for the first eleven of the thirteen number programme: without any musical accompaniment, it relied on the Conductor's tuning fork and a firm right arm to start them all off on the same note and at the same time.

Happily, this aspect of their performance couldn't be faulted.

They all started and finished together.

The storks, nesting in huge bundles of twigs on the church bell-tower (as they did along much of the Camino), relieved the monotony from time to time by clacking their beaks like castanets as the conductor was about to launch another number.

Instead of Basque music, which would have been fantastic, the choir had planned a programme to suit every nation but without understanding the interpretation that would have brought it to life.

Technically brilliant, it was spiritually bereft.

I've never heard an Irish folk song performed like a dirge: and I'm sure that people from Germany, France, Cuba, Colombia and Argentina would have made similar comments about their own tribute songs.

But when they finished with a couple of Basque songs, their faces lit up and they really looked as if they were happy, and not just at the imminent prospect of something to eat and drink.

So the obligatory encores were merited, in the end.

Sandwiches and rolls followed, with universal fillings in which mayonnaise featured prominently. And wine, of course.

I found the *panadería*, about which The Bronzed German Cyclist had told me, still open almost opposite the Refuge: I ended up sitting outside in the alley with a can of Coke, for which I'd developed an insatiable craving, and an orange, listening to the choir again but this time in their natural environment.

Now, they were in their civvies and well lubricated by alcohol: they broke into spontaneous song, and they were brilliant. They led a fantastic singalong.

When they left, we were full of a rosy glow for Basque music: if there had been a CD for sale, I'd probably have bought it but only if it hadn't been rehearsed to death.

I got to bed late at about 10.30: a non-music loving, non-partying pilgrim grimly snapped off the light, and so I couldn't pack properly. My own fault.

Day 9
Logroño to Navarrete
10 km   598 km to go

Come the morning, I felt very below par: walking would be an effort, I felt, and it was.

3 km of concrete road from Logroño: then a rocky path which made my battered feet wince at every step. I reached Navarrete after 10 km in four hours, and every step was a drag.

Lack of food, liquid, salt? Or just general fatigue after eight long days?

It was Sunday.

I stopped for a drink and a *sello* at a table set up by the

Amigos de Camino in the car park beside the lake in the park outside Logroño.

'Looks like rain' (well actually, with my restricted Spanish vocabulary, I probably said something like 'Lluvia pronto?' (rain soon?) I remarked cheerily to the *sello*-ist, pointing at the ominously black sky.

He laughed as the first heavy drops of rain fell.

'No rain today', he said.

I practised putting the cover on my rucksack and ripping my raintop from it's handy sack.

It rained for an hour.

The footpath, fenced off on one side from a wood chipping factory, was separated from the main road on the other side by a chain link fence. Pilgrims had made crosses from the long chips of wood which had been blasted through from the woodyard, and fixed them into the fence beneath the lowering gaze of one of the ninety remaining Veterano Osborne advertising bulls from the

Pilgrim crosses beside the woodyard

*Tired pilgrims waiting for opening time at Navarrete:
less tired pilgrims at the bar in the background*

hillside above. Now, I understand, they are protected: but years ago, they towered over every road through Spain.

Do you remember them, or even the drink?

Dates me, I suppose: I felt an instant urge to get stuck into a bottle **now,** or at the very least, as soon as I got home.

I felt totally drained when I reached the Refuge: a number of equally weary pilgrims were sitting hunched beneath the cloisters of this beautiful mediaeval town, beside the door.

The order of preference was posted on the door, to weed out the less needy:

1 Pilgrims on foot who had come from Los Arcos or Torres del Rio

2 Pilgrims in need of medical assistance (Me, please, sir! Look at my feet!)

3 Pilgrims who had left Logroño after 4 pm. (It would be 7pm before they arrived, and the chances of a Hospitalero prizing a pilgrim from his bunk to make room for such a deserving cause would be nil – or even less!)

4 Pilgrims on bicycles

It didn't mention pilgrims who had started from Logroño at dawn: in the event of a struggle, I would appear to rank below even the cyclists!

It was like the order of preference on the signboard outside Izikiah O'Donovan's lodging house in Cornwall many years ago.

I quote it in full: that's what it was like in Cornwall (and probably elsewhere, I hasten to add) before equal opportunities legislation came into force.

There's no doubt that, nowadays, he'd be sued by every razor grinder in the business.

> RULES OF THIS LODGING HOUSE
> Fourpence a night for bed (1.7p)
> Sixpence with supper (2.5p)
> No more than three to sleep in one bed
> No beer allowed in the kitchen
> No smoking when in bed
> No Clothes to be washed on Sunday
> No Boots to be worn in bed
> No Dogs allowed upstairs
> No Gambling or Fighting here
> No extra charge for Luggage
> No Razor Grinders taken in
> Organ Grinders to sleep in the attick
> By
> IZIKIAH O'DONOVAN

Donkeys, Chaises, Handcarts and Durries Let on Hire
MANGLING DONE HERE

And let me tell you, half of these rules still apply in the Refuges in Spain (thank goodness)!

Presumably, razor grinders were trouble: I'm sure that this doesn't apply to cyclists at the Navarrete Refuge.

I left my rucksack under the arches, and went off to follow the music that I could hear. Yes, you could leave your rucksack safely amidst the other pilgrims in Spanish villages along the Camino: but I kept my papers firmly fixed round my waist in my bumbag. There is a limit to trust!

A Mediaeval Fair (spelt 'Fayre' in Southern England) was in full swing: I asked the Tourist Office in the square what it was all about, but the young lady on duty didn't know.

Basque music was being played on drums and flutes: a lady stilt walker was doing impossible twists and twirls on 18 inch (45 cm) high stilts on the uneven cobbles, and dancers were cavorting around in a mediaeval sort of way.

Stalls sold country food: a man was making Spanish musical instruments: jewellery stalls abounded: cheap cider, at €1 a glass, and probably (judging by the cloudy content) straight from the bucket, had a kick like a team of mules.

Was it the Maharishi selling intricate bracelets that expanded into all sorts of symmetrical shapes from a table in the corner?

Probably not, I decided, although he had the tools on the table at his side and claimed that he made the bracelets himself in the long winter evenings (and there were plenty of these high up in this part of Spain, where winters were as bitterly cold as the summers were hot). I guessed that they had been probably imported from India.

I was fascinated by them: €6 each. How much; €60? No, no, €6.

I was so fascinated (I get these critically unsupportable urges), I would probably have paid €60 in an insane moment until I worked out that this would be over £40. Sanity prevailed: but I still bought a handful of these (probably) Indian or Nepalese bracelets as presents from Spain for my family and friends.

And who should be inspecting the stall of wooden puzzles (on the lines of Rubik Cubes, which not surprisingly turned out to have been his favourite toy as a child) but Benoit!

He had wandered in from somewhere: now he was about to wander out.

A man who looked as Wurzel Gummidge might have looked if he'd neglected himself for a year or two, had a bicycle festooned with amazing impedimenta.

He was playing flute, bagpipes and accordion with accompanying taped animal noises.

I spoke to him afterwards, to say what amazing music he was playing. It turned out that he'd lived in England for fourteen years, latterly in Brighton where he'd been at the time of the Brighton Bombing: he'd trained as a juggler, and with a group of other trainee jugglers, Pedro (yes, that's his name) had performed at a Gala Dinner for Prince Edward.

He wouldn't go into details, but apparently the performance had left something to be desired: although they were ushered to the door in the end they had, said Pedro, been paid!

He had appeared in Covent Garden (the now upmarket former Fruit and Vegetable Market, not the swanky modern theatre) and on television: now he worked his way round the Mediaeval Fairs in Spain, the Basque areas of France, and Slovenia.

He gave me his leaflet: if I was in his area, especially if I had any problems, I was to call.

He lived, he assured me, in quite a nice area.

I asked if he also did weddings, funerals, parties and Bar Mitzvahs.

Pedro, star of the medieval fair at Navarrete

He shook his head. No, Country Festivals kept him busy. Ah, Wurzel, another illusion shattered. But I wasn't surprised. He's a class act.

I'd thought that he and the Lady on the Stilts with her supporting troupe were just itinerant musicians, or talented local amateurs doing a charity gig for the day.

No, he had an agent who organised his bookings and took a percentage.

The next time I saw him, he was sitting at a shady table making out his returns for his agent, who was enjoying a nourishing mixed salad outside the market pub.

The musicians were a theatrical troupe: and no, they weren't playing authentic mediaeval Basque music, but Basque **type** music which they'd composed themselves and which sounded, well, **right**!

They were accomplished tumblers, rounding off the Fayre (sorry, Fair) with a tumbling display to their own 'Basque' music before a wildly enthusiastic crowd: families in their Sunday best at the annual Country Market at the end of July.

Maggie, the **Canadian** clairvoyant of Venezuelan extraction with horrifying rucksack burns across shoulders and back (and on medication for various other ailments picked up already along the Camino: she could rarely start before 1000 because she'd become a fixture in sympathetic doctor's surgeries all the way from St Jean), who I'd met at Logroño, turned up at the Refuge.

She'd teamed up with Renata, the **Austrian** clairvoyant who'd received a message at Easter that she had to walk the Camino (do you remember? Oh, never mind!), along the way. Renata looked surprisingly fresh and well after 23 km from Viana.

I guess that, both being clairvoyants, they'd known that they were going to meet: and, having met, there was no reason to talk because I assume that they knew what each other was going to say and what the reply would be.

So they chattered about mundane things and seemed happy.

I had an upper bunk for the first time: eight ladies and two men in our palatial five star dormitory, sharing two showers, two toilets and two washbasins.

The Unchristian Theoretically Christian Spanish Lady was in the next bunk.

She told me that she and her friend were finishing their pilgrimage for this year that night, and would go on to Santo Domingo de la Calzada by bus on the way home tomorrow.

'Will you stay in the Refuge tomorrow night?'

'Oh yes'.

I hoped that they would give up their bunks if a couple of weary pilgrims arrived late (me, for instance): but somehow, I feared that they might not. It's all a matter of priorities.

But next morning, after my perilous descent from the top

bunk, swaying on one leg to pull on my socks to avoid invading her space by sitting on her, she patted the corner of her bunk for me to sit down and pull on socks and shoes in comfort. Perhaps she wasn't all **that** bad, after all.

It was obviously a prosperous town, because there was a palatial kitchen in the Refuge: in many 'poorer' areas, such as Galicia, Refuge kitchens were either basic or didn't exist so that pilgrims would spend money in local shops and bars out of necessity and so boost the local economy. Of course, that's how it had all started a thousand years ago: small communities had arisen beside the Camino for just that reason.

In fact, the kitchen was huge, with lots of polished MFI type tables, a washing machine, spin drier and oven – and a MICROWAVE. However, we were instructed that these were not all to be used at the same time: I guess that the power surge would have blown up most of the town.

The young Hospitalero and his girlfriend, who couldn't keep their hands off each other (it was rather sweet, but quite exhausting even for onlookers) and spent most of the afternoon in close contact, operated from a corner of the kitchen where they stamped the *sellos* and allotted the bunks and, presumably, cross examined pilgrims to see where and when they'd started (Logroño at 3.45pm? Back of the queue behind the cyclists, I'm afraid).

Nobody appeared embarrassed.

A sunburnt Englishman, whose skin appeared to have been through some sort of tanning process, told me that he was on his way back to Le Puy (a round trip of 2,990 km!). He might have been about my age: on the other hand, he might have been about 50: it's amazing what the Camino will do to your looks.

He'd arrived late: the walking had turned out easier than he'd thought and, as he had plenty of time in hand, thought he'd walk back as well. How far each day?

'Oh, forty, up to fifty kilometres a day' he said nonchalantly.

I gasped and clutched the table, sipping the hot sweet tea that a pilgrim, possibly aware of this imminent shock, had just provided.

'Had you trained?' he asked me.

'Oh, yes, on the South Downs'.

'That's plenty of ups and downs' (no, it **wasn't** a joke!), he said: 'I just walked round our farm in Norfolk each day: mind you, it's quite large.'

After I tore myself away from the Fair, I'd rushed into the Café/Bar next door for an enticingly billed 'toasted cheese and ham sandwich'.

It turned out to be cold ham and cold slices of plastic cheese between two slices of thick toast made from sweet cake bread (which I **hate** anyway!) and which now ranks high on my list of nauseating meals. I donated most of it to the starving dogs of Navarrete.

I went back to the Refuge and dug out my antistarvation insurance policy from the depths of my rucksack, a packet of tomato soup.

I added some rice from the Pilgrim Reserve Collection Of Old Food from the kitchen cupboard.

I'd never used an electric cooker before, so I boiled it up on maximum, Number 6.

Then, as I would with gas, I turned it down to Number 1 to simmer.

Didn't work. Still kept boiling. The top of the cooker was soon covered with congealing tomato soup and rapidly hardening rice.

I'd eaten two bowls of this thickening mixture (well, how was

I to know the extent to which rice would expand?), with some plasticised bread left over from the previous evening in Logroño, before the top of the cooker had cooled.

Even the scouring pad was singed.

I surreptitiously poured away the remaining bucketful of tomato flavoured rice.

After a couple of hours for recovery, I went back to the Bar/Restaurant for macaroni and tomato sauce, but this time with lumps of spicy chorizo sausage: a perfect snack before bed.

Bed early: I'd had (by Camino standards) an exciting day.

17 km to Nájera tomorrow: and I must try to keep to my projected schedule because little slack time remains now. 172 km in nine days to date: 588 km in a maximum 33 days ahead.

4

Enter Popeye and The Gloucester Girls

Day 10
Navarrete to Nájera
17 km   588 km to go

Breakfast on the house: wow!

Hot chocolate, made with cold milk, bread, jam and butter: and off at 0700 through the cloisters and the narrow streets of this little mediaeval town.

Only eleven miles planned: this was the last of my ten days 'walking-in', and time to step up my mileage (well, what other words could I use?)

The first 5 km were along the road, dodging juggernauts: but after this, I strolled along the steep footpaths through the open countryside and lonely vineyards, bordered for the first 2 km with piles of stones piled one on one erected by pilgrims as symbols of prayer and often stretching far up the hillsides.

I spent half an hour fascinated by a huge ant's nest (no, should be 'huge ant nest', because the ants were **actually** normal size).

They were dragging grass and wheat seeds to the entrance hole of their nest, which was surrounded by the empty husks.

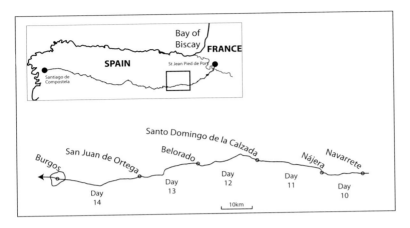

Probably like the Harvester Ants of Death Valley, where the seeds were 'milled' by the workers, and the ground seeds regurgitated and fed to the larvae deep within the nest.

When I at last looked up, I found that I was almost in the shadow of the circular hill, the Poyo Roldán, where Roland is said to have slain the Syrian giant Ferragut with a huge stone, a trick that he must have learnt from David when he beat Goliath 1-0.

The final 4 km through the outskirts of a rapidly developing Nájera were brightened by the 'Poem of the Camino', in Castilian with German translation, on the long wall of a huge factory beside the footpath. No, I couldn't understand a word of it: but I'm lucky, because I've got an English translation!

The Camino was impeccably signposted through the town: the clatter of storks on the church towers accompanied me through the streets to the wonderfully modern Refuge in the Monastery in the centre of town. They'd done a great conversion job: 50 bunks, two toilets, two showers, a kitchen cum washroom with two sinks to wash your kit – and all for only €3!

It's split level and open plan, in bright pale wood: only

drawback, all the washing has to be pegged on two revolving driers fixed outside the two upstairs windows, and if it drops down into the yard, I'm not sure how you'd get it back.

Popeye (Popeye? Yes, you know, after the Seaman. I hope I've spelt it right), a young, blonde, languid German, was busy cremating a pan of potato and onion as I washed my towel in the sink at his side.

Had I got any pepper, he wondered? No, I admitted, it was one of the things that I had sadly omitted to bring.

Popeye was only walking the Camino as far as León, where he was meeting up with people building a commune so that he could help.

September or October (he seemed unsure which), he had to return to Germany to do his National Service, either nine months in the armed forces, or ten months doing Social Services.

He was going to work in a kindergarten.

He was pretty laidback about it: they very often released you early if you had a good reason, because they were short of money.

He and a group of friends had driven from San Sebastian to Pamplona, where they had bought a donkey and set off with it to walk the Camino.

As the donkey could only manage six to eight kilometres a day, it was quite a slow process.

Whenever they reached a town, they would stay for two or three days, juggling and doing tricks and performing in the street (he seemed a little vague about the content of the show) to raise money to sustain the donkey.

But after about three weeks, the others had set off back to Pamplona to get the necessary papers to take the donkey back to Germany, leaving him to walk the Camino alone to León.

His friends were going to walk with the donkey all the way to

Berlin, which seemed rather a long term commitment on both sides.

When I got back from my trip to the Supermarket, Popeye was juggling with four big clubs in the square outside the Monastery (Refuge).

He seemed to drop them quite regularly, although he also had good spells of several seconds when your hopes rose quite rapidly.

Nevertheless, I hope that he was the one that went round with the hat when the group were performing in the street to raise enough cash to support the donkey. Otherwise, they would have been hard put even to reach subsistence level.

Still, I guess even Pedro had to start **somewhere:** and now look at **him**!

I had a pilgrim meal nearby: the restaurant proprietor had been distributing leaflets outside the Refuge as we sat waiting for admittance, and it seemed only right to encourage her. Meals were billed to start at 7pm: at 7.45, they weren't **quite** ready to open, but it all seemed quite good humoured.

€8: about £5. Seemed a bit expensive: but what the heck! Sometimes, you feel like splashing out on an expensive restaurant.

Macaroni was off (and I was the first in!): but I had an enormous plate of (yes, you've guessed it!) spaghetti and tomato sauce spangled with thin slices of chorizo. The fish that followed was – well, just fish. No veg – just, well, half a fish split lengthwise.

It gazed reproachfully up at me: you could see that, not long ago, it had been a real one doing some relaxing swimming.

The other half had obviously gone to another pilgrim.

I hope he enjoyed it: I had to throw most of mine away. It had probably been anorexic, which was why it had succumbed so easily after starving itself to skin and bone.

The chocolate tart was beautifully firm textured: some would have said dry, but if you'd been lying around the kitchen for a day or so, **you'd** be a bit dry too.

Wine: ah good, it was already uncorked, straight from the tanker.

I resisted most of it and wandered back to the Refuge.

Too late to pack ready for the morning, and anyway the bunks were so close together that you'd end up packing for everybody else. Synchronised packing was called for.

Day 11
Nájera to Santo Domingo de la Calzada
23 km   571 km to go

Tactics demanded a 5.30 lunge for the facilities.

I was ahead of the field, and almost in pole position for breakfast.

Tepid milk (no danger of an insurance claim for scalding yourself with boiling milk), to which you added the powder of your choice: sweet biscuits, sponge fingers, plastic bread and my remaining orange and yoghourt made a very satisfying meal.

I was set up for the day. Quick packing in the still dark dormitory, full of pilgrims blundering about in the dark, fearful of turning on the light.

The first few kilometres were on road through the town, giving a firm pothole-less footing in the dark: the sun rose as the off-road track was reached, and then came wonderful walking through the dry, red hills. The Guide Book had threatened a 'ravine', which had kept me awake quaking for half the night. Actually, it was rather a jolly sort of hilly rift between the hills.

I passed Renata standing in one of the shady bits, looking a bit forlorn. Yes, she was alright: just suffering from feet and heat.

We walked along together, and entered the fertile valley around Azófra: for the first time, intensive irrigation systems were whisking water around busily, and it looked a very productive, even affluent, market gardening area.

Azófra itself boasted a Refuge in the main square, opposite the shady fountain: more importantly for me, it also boasted a sleek chrome trimmed shady coffee bar which,, even at 8 a.m., was packed with pilgrims.

I rushed in for a café con leche grande fix: can't get enough of it at present, wonder if I'll change when I get home because I can't **stand** coffee!

Perhaps it's all part of a midlife personality change, or a late male menopause, and I'll become a new man and nice to know!

I sat around, putting off the non-stop 16 km drag that lay ahead.

OK, let's go: 08.22, and the sun already getting high in the sky and looking for potential victims.

Renata stayed behind for a few more minutes: both of us, I think, like to walk alone.

I kept up my 100 paces a minute for the next hour and a half. Now come on, who says that I'm boring? Got to keep my mind active along the firm straight stony track. Now, where was I? Oh yes: one, two, three, four – dash, I stopped to look at an interesting ant, was it eighty six or eighty seven?

I can't keep it up: so many views to stop and admire, plants to look at, interesting things around in this wonderful part of the world that I will perhaps never visit again.

Photographs evoke memories as well, and I take lots of them.

A long hill should have led me to Cirueña; but we were directed to make a long detour for 'Security Reasons' round a vast area, segregated by a tall forbidding chain link fence.

Was it, perhaps, a top secret Nuclear Power Plant?

No, folks, it was the Rioja Alta golf course. Wait, it's no use grabbing your clubs and dashing for the plane, because it's not open yet: but the lush fairways, satin greens and opulent buildings hint at unimaginable delights to come.

And when you drive off from the first tee at some time in the distant future, remember who told you about it first.

Santo Domingo de la Calzada has so far mercifully resisted over-modernisation. It's another town through which we used to drive in the old days: and like all good places, it's got lots of great stories.

It's a gratifying tribute to 'local boy makes good'.

Way back in the eleventh century, Domingo (a shepherd) wanted to enter the monastery of San Millán de Cogilla: but he was refused admission because he was illiterate.

So he built a hermitage and chapel in the forest in a particularly bandit-infested stretch of the Camino to care for pilgrims between Logroño and Burgos. He built a Hospital (it's a Parador now, and you know how upmarket **they** are which would probably have rejected a modern-day Domingo for not having enough credit cards or a four wheel drive car) in the town that now bears his name, and a causeway and a bridge over the river Oja (Rio oja – Rioja, get it? Oh well, never mind: who says I never try to educate people?) and devoted the rest of his long ninety year life to road and bridge building. One of his disciples, San Juan de Ortega, carried on where Domingo had left off and **he** had a town named after himself as well!

No, we've not finished our stories yet.

There's a magnificent cathedral in the town, where Domingo was buried: and high up in the building is an ornate gilded cage containing a very much alive cockerel and hen.

Animal lovers will be pleased to know that these are donated, and replaced every month, and whilst they are there receive a very good nourishing diet: I can tell you, conditions are far better than those of the average battery chicken. But that's beside the point: we're getting away from the story.

A family of three pilgrims stayed at an inn in the town almost seven hundred years ago. The girl at the inn took a fancy to their eighteen year old son, Hugonell: and when her advances were rejected, she 'planted' a silver goblet in his luggage and after the family had left, denounced him to the authorities.

The punishment for robbery was death: and the unfortunate Hugonell was hanged for a crime that he had never committed.

His parents completed the pilgrimage and, on the return journey, found him there alive although still hanging, with his feet supported by St James. So they went to see the judge and told him of their son's innocence. The judge was just sitting down to a hearty dinner, and said scornfully something along the lines that the boy was no more likely to be innocent than the cock and hen on his plate were to get up and fly.

At which, the cock and hen flew away, as proof of their son's innocence.

So in memory of this event a live cock and hen, always white, are kept in this gilded cage: and opposite the niche commemorating

The cock and hen at Santo Domingo de la Calzada

this miracle is a piece of wood from the gallows on which the unfortunate Hugonell was hanged.

An indulgence is granted to all who devoutly walk around the Saint's tomb reciting Our Father, Hail Mary and Gloria.

I was limping along, following the *flechas* through the town to the Albergue Peregrino (Pilgrim Refuge, I never know whether to call it an Albergue or Refugio, so I'll carry on calling it 'The Refuge') when I had an enormous stroke of good fortune.

I saw a pilgrim walking out of an old building.

It was! It was! It was the Refuge at the old Cistercian Nunnery, a 'must' to visit. Most of the first 30+ pilgrims had all walked past in their quest for the municipal Refuge further up the street.

Good job, because there were only 21 bunks there: and apart from an English Family On A Walking Holiday (all the way from Roncesvalles to Santiago, actually) and a French couple, I was the only other pilgrim to have arrived!

I went under the archway and into a dark corridor, at the end of which was a small reception booth.

A compact elderly nun, who had to stand on tiptoe to make eye contact through the glass screen above the waist high counter, addressed me in Spanish.

She looked like a teller in a nunnery bank.

Was this the place that I'd heard about where pilgrims slept on mattresses on the floor?

No, said the English Gentleman On A Walking Holiday who happened to be passing, they'd just been given a guided tour by another compact elderly nun, it was superb.

'Yes please, me next' I almost shouted at the elderly nun, thrusting my Pilgrim Passport across the counter.

Through the cool vaulted lobby and up the well worn stone stairs: and there were three tiny bedrooms, bunks with room to sit up on the bottom bunk without lacerating the top of your head, and each with a coverlet rather like a threadbare version of the candlewick bedspreads of my youth.

I was first in: and I had a bottom bunk!

I sprawled on my cool shady bunk, relaxing after the heat of the Camino, as the other pilgrims sharing the six bedded dormitory arrived one by one.

Renata made it, just as the afternoon roast began, with her voluptuous friend Anita (also from Austria) who similarly spoke perfect English: Richard from Southend: and another lady whose name I don't know. Sorry, unknown lady.

Oh yes: and Popeye.

Popeye? Yes, somehow he'd rolled up at the nunnery. The side pockets of his huge rucksack bulged with his four juggling batons, a bit scarred from regular contact with the concrete (he wasn't, you may recall, the world's greatest juggler): whilst an enormous battered didgeridoo poked out of the top.

Perhaps **this** had been the musical centrepiece of the touring ensemble which had been assembled to sustain the donkey: had I wronged him by suggesting that he was a juggler poor and simple?

The Refuge at the nunnery was superb: three toilets, three showers which lent a fresh meaning to 'power wash' (all unisex as usual: after a week on the Camino, you lose most of your inhibitions), and an enormous low beamed refectory (with a tiny two ring cooker in the corner) with a huge open fireplace.

A door led into a garden filled with roses, shady trees and loads of drying frames and lines.

I could have kissed the dear old nun who had guided me round: but I thought that, under the circumstances, this might not go down too well.

So I contented myself with giving her a generous donation

(Does €5 seem too much to pay for such luxury?). But not **too** much, or it will increase expectations and could lead to galloping inflation along the Camino.

The previous (and only) time I stayed in a nunnery in Spain, or anywhere else come to that, was when Felbridge Juniors Rugby Club played in San Sebastian, and Dick Griffiths had to be supported up the stone stairs, leaning backwards at an angle of 45 degrees, to the amazement of the watching nuns. He was, you understand, tired and emotional: but that, as they say, is another story.

Might cook a meal now. How about spaghetti or macaroni, and some tomato sauce? Now **there's** a good idea!

I wandered round the tiny *supermercado*, trying to find just enough spaghetti or macaroni for one, and a packet or two of tomato sauce. I gave up and bought a fat baguette, some cheese and a packet of sweaty salami for breakfast.

I took them with me to the cathedral, to explore the legend of the cock and the hen. The cathedral museum closed at 6.30: so I dashed back to warn Renata.

We took our Pilgrim Passports and got another *sello*, and reduced entry to the cathedral museum because of our pilgrim status, €1.5 as against €2.

The cathedral is just fantastic: whilst the hen and cock looked very healthy.

We got another *sello* at the Tourist Office: Renata went to the service at the cathedral, and I went to get a meal.

The romantic idea of cooking my own meal in the low beamed refectory at the nunnery on the primitive cooker was abandoned.

I settled for a big plate of macaroni, bread and wine in a bar round the corner from the nunnery.

That evening Richard From Southend and myself sat in the nunnery garden, chatting with two statuesque young lady students from Slovenia, There is an organisation for students over there, they told us, which enables them to travel very cheaply to far flung areas of Europe in long distance lorries, sat up front with the driver: although demand is high at this time of year (it had taken them a fortnight on the internet to make arrangements for the two day trip), it had enabled them to travel all the way to Spain for only €50 (and the truckers had waived the charge anyway).

They were going to link up again with the website when they reached Santiago and return by the same route: although they might take a few days off on a beach somewhere first.

Inevitably, talk turned to wars and the part played by religion.

Even today, one of them said, there are villages in Slovenia where Muslims live on one side of the road and Orthodox (she thought, might have been wrong) on the other, and they daren't even cross the centre of the road to visit other family members.

What a tragedy in the name of religion: tolerance was fine, as long as you worship **my** way.

Popeye was entertaining a young lady pilgrim on the shaded patio.

They had already demolished one bottle of wine and were well on their way through a second. The young lady informed me that she was intending to accompany Popeye along the Camino, playing the spoons as he performed on the didgeridoo. She gave a demonstration.

With a little polishing, the act could stun audiences all the way to Santiago: and, had there been the added attraction of a donkey, the potential seemed limitless.

Just then an elderly nun appeared, gesturing that it was five to ten and hinting that all good pilgrims should be heading for bed.

Popeye bent forward to listen: he wasn't very tall, but the nun was minute.

Was there a height limit on new recruits at this particular nunnery: did they have to be able to walk beneath a bar, like children at the Bouncy Castle at our local Sports Centre, to gain admission?

Did taller nuns go elsewhere?

Was there a special Convent for nuns of 6 ft plus, high in the Sierra Nevada?

Popeye sighed, faced with the inevitable, and reluctantly went up to bed, clutching his bottle.

The Lady Spoon Player trailed off elsewhere.

Popeye, holding on to his bunk to remain stable, delivered a brief but passionate diatribe to the rest of the dormitory, who appeared unmoved.

'It was ridiculous', he said, 'to come to bed so early': when all he wanted to do was to sit around on this beautiful warm evening, drink a little wine, indulge in deep meaningful conversation (well, that's what he meant, but his command of English wasn't quite up to it) and generally relax.

He was, he said, rather…, what was the word?

I think 'pissed off' summed it up best: but suggested 'annoyed', which seemed to go down quite well.

He'd lost the cork from the bottle: telling me to take care not to knock it over, he placed it carefully between my shoes and scaled the top bunk where he fell asleep before we could even turn out the light.

Day 12
Santo Domingo de la Calzada to Belorado
23 km   548 km to go

Everybody slept well: nobody was making tactical toilet trips, and nobody awoke until after 6.00. That's what a small dormitory of tired pilgrims **should** be like.

I was packed, had my breakfast (an orange, and stale bread scraped in Primula) and left by 6.43.

Popeye had just stirred: what was the time?

The English Family On A Walking Holiday were still asleep in the next dormitory.

All was peaceful: a Nunnery at rest.

It was so peaceful that many pilgrims were reluctant to leave at all.

Apparently the Nun's tactics soon changed, from what I heard later.

Instead of the dear old pocket-sized nun who had gently chided Popeye for lingering in the garden, they released 'Sister Agatha'.

She would never have got under the gate of the Bouncy Castle.

'O.K. you lot! Get out NOW!' was the gist of her message.

She'd obviously been released from the back room, where she'd been simmering on a diet of iron filings and toning up on intensive weight training, as their secret weapon: and by the 08.00 deadline, the remaining pilgrims had been bundled out into the street and the nunnery returned to peace.

I'd already been on my way for an hour and a half in the cool morning air, breathing in the heady fumes of clapped-out builder's lorries shuddering into action. I strode through the outskirts of Santo Domingo de la Calzada and over the bridge across the Rio Oja.

After a few kilometres I caught up with the Lady Spoon Player, who had obviously abandoned the idea of a show business career.

She was sauntering along with a couple of Spaniards.

It was a golden world as far as the eye could see, surrounded by a rim of violet mountains. The stony track of the Camino seemed unending.

I stopped for a café con leche grande at Grañón, at a bar in a narrow stone paved street opposite the church. I sat somewhat hesitantly with the Gloucester Girls, who'd shared my space at Nájera.

'Hesitantly', because yesterday they'd come upon me unawares as I was having a quiet pee at the edge of a cornfield beside the Camino, contemplating the distant mountains and ruminating on the vastness of nature.

Fortunately, I'd had my back turned: but they'd stopped for a chat with each other immediately behind me.

I hadn't seen them at Santo Domingo, where they'd slept at the large Municipal Refuge: but they seemed alright about it, one of them took my photo sitting at rest outside the bar.

Guess I'll only know what they thought about me when I get the prints back and find out whether she'd cut off my head.

I could hear their tinkling laughter behind me along the Camino as they cross examined a young Spaniard with two heavily bandaged knees.

Through Redecilla del Camino and Castildelgado, which had all the hallmarks of an abandoned village.

An old man was sitting on an old bench beneath an old vine outside an old house, doing something with pieces of straw. A dog barked. But Villamajor del Río, 5 km down the road, obviously had aspirations of becoming one of the holiday centres of north west Spain.

A brand new Albergue with room for 52 pilgrims and lots of showers and toilets was already in full swing: and local economy was set to boom.

But it was too close to Belorado, a nice day's walk (23 km) from Santo Domingo.

I was beginning to stride out, aware that the guide book warned that there were only 20 pilgrim places in the Refuge built into the wall of the church, although there was also the potential to sleep on the Ayuntiamento (Town Hall) floor.

But there was another new Albergue (Refuge) in Belorado. The Cuatro Cantones had been opened a year ago by a family from Burgos and was now so successful that father and mother might even move back to Burgos and probably start the next link in a chain of Refuges.

Cuatro Cantones was sheer luxury.

For instance, the polished wooden bunks had ladders to the top bunks, instead of wriggling your toes under someone's armpit and swinging your free leg onto the top mattress: and once again, you could sit upright on the bottom bunk without causing severe lacerations to your head.

The showers and toilets, washrooms and sinks, had been carefully planned and gleamed crystal white. Sixty pilgrims could sleep in comfort, and there was a large kitchen and **free** tea and coffee (and some cakes if you arrived early, which I did: in fact, they were so good that I arrived **twice**).

And the family were great: they all smiled and made you welcome, and seemed genuinely pleased to see you. So, five star Albergue: but you know, I still wished that I'd experienced the old Refuge in the church wall where you do your washing on top of the vault! Never satisfied, are we?

I discussed it all over a cup of herbal tea with the Slovenian

Girls and a Former French Ballet Dancer Now Living In Germany who'd just launched her own website.

She draped herself artistically over the computer screen in the lobby, Belorado's own Internet café, proudly showing off her website to any pilgrim who might happen to be passing.

Murphy's Bar in the nearby Calle Gral Mola, where I'd hoped to be served with a Guinness by Murphy himself, was the only Irish pub I'd ever met that remained inexplicably closed throughout the day and evening.

So I decided to find the other Refuge.

Turned out that I'd walked past it on the way to Cuatro Cantones: one time that my famed ability to lose my way had paid off.

It was run by a Swiss group of Amigos de Camino. It was already full.

So was the overflow building across the road, where I almost knocked over a stack of three tier bunks laden with resting pilgrims, which swayed perilously when I opened the back door by mistake.

Who should I find but Renata, Maggie and her Spanish friend, the Swedish couple (her sister had already returned), the Gloucester Girls and the English Roses!

Renata and Maggie were just about to eat: macaroni and tomato sauce, of course, plus salad and followed by fruit and cream.

Would I like to join them? Would I!

I gorged myself fully, only to find that I had to do my share of the washing-up with Renata.

Had nobody told Austrian and Canadian of Venezuelan extraction women that English men just **don't** wash up, never mind cook!

But I put on a brave face, hoped that nobody I knew would

see me, and dropped nothing. Actually, I almost enjoyed it: it was quite therapeutic.

Back to the garden of the Cuatro Cantones, where I lounged in a chair beneath a fig tree, watching the washing dry and sipping a coke. What could be more perfect?

The idyll was broken by the arrival of Renata and Maggie (who one day hoped to become an astrologer as well).

They hadn't believed my stories of how good it was here (surely, as clairvoyants, they should have known?): they departed suitably chastened and, what's more, they realised that I was half a kilometre nearer to Santiago than them.

Aileen turned up on her bicycle, riding from Santiago to France. She'd decided to go cycling on the Continent for the summer, and hadn't heard about the Camino until she'd read an article in a Spanish newspaper (good job she could read Spanish).

'Where do you think I come from?', she said.

I hazarded Durham: then I thought that it might be the USA.

Turned out to be Edinburgh: but that was alright, she said, because it was a very distinctive accent and not all that many people lived there anyway.

All my Scots friends fitted a harsher Glasgow stereotype.

She couldn't get over the contrast between the age old life of Spain and modern Spain: how, riding along the gleaming hi-tec roads of Galicia, valleys crossed by huge concrete multi-arch bridges, she had seen little hunched old ladies in black beside the road, who she likened to the villagers of mountainous Bolivia (yes, she **had** been there herself!), as an incongruous contrast between their lifestyle of (being charitable) sixty years ago and which still existed into the 1970s, and the present day.

As I entered Galicia a fortnight later, I was to see this at first hand as I peered into the shady doorways of the farmyards bordering the village streets, breathing in the sweet smell of the cattle, with long-lashed cows wandering along the 'main road' at their own pace to find their own stalls, and guided by hunched old ladies in green wellies who gently prodded them along with a hazel stick. Fifty metres further along might be a modern upmarket house, with a gleaming four wheel drive car outside, a status symbol for the thrusting young executive from the city who revelled in his country pad: and next door would be a dilapidated cottage, with a vine above the doorway.

Lights out just sort of happened by mutual consent at around 10.30.

Popeye would have been in his element and in this super laidback Albergue could have entertained until the small hours on his didgeridoo, probably juggling at the same time.

I had acres of space to pack for the morning.

5

The Mountains, the Monastery and Atapuerca Man

Day 13
Belorado to San Juan de Ortega
24 km   525 km to go

Up at 5.30: breakfast on the house, and as usual I wandered around wasting time.

I set off at 6.15 and promptly lost my way, meandered round the bandstand in the square, and suddenly found myself passing Murphy's Bar and then the Cuatro Cantones once again just as the English Roses came past. I tagged along until we'd passed the blocks of flats on the edge of town, and it was difficult for even **me** to lose my way after that.

The first 3 km were difficult walking: pointy stones that made me gasp whenever my right foot landed on a particularly nasty one. But it was well marked and undemanding: and the overcast sky and the mist covered mountains not only kept it cool, but also worried me about the prospect of rain. That's nothing new, of course: I **always** worry about the prospect of rain.

I reached Villafranca Montes de Oca (11 km) in less than

three hours. Well, I **am** The Slowest Pilgrim.

Café con leche grande and tortilla at the big Café/Bar where three roads meet at the entrance to the village.

Now, tortilla sounds far better than it usually is. Here, it was a huge nauseous rapidly congealing plasticised slab of potato faintly tinged with the taste of egg: I folded some of it up and put it in my rucksack for later.

But there was only just over 500 km to Santiago: 33% gone, and I was feeling good.

Even my feet had perked up.

2.5 km later, and this 'feeling good' feeling was being rapidly diluted.

Turn right beside the church: and then there is a long steep narrow stony track to the Fuente de Mojapan. Apparently, this means 'Moisten bread' and it's where pilgrims would shelter because the area ahead, through the woods on the foothills of the Montes de Oca, was too dangerous to cross at night and anyway there were lots of wolves around.

I tell you, it was hard work being a pilgrim in the Middle Ages: and **we** worry about blisters, and lack of paper in the toilets.

Now there were picnic tables beside the track: and the Gloucester Girls and their tame Spaniard with the bandaged knees, Francesc, were in possession.

The Gloucester Girls, cousins and eighteen years old, as usual when we met on these steep climbs asked me solicitously 'Are you **alright?**' like nieces looking after an elderly uncle. Francesc beamed and gave his usual 'Hel-**lo**'.

It was a pity that I was forced to pass them: I liked to keep them well ahead of me, because I was still mildly paranoid about the prospect of them passing me unawares once again in full flow.

On the pinnacle of the mountain stands an impressive monument, the Monumento de los Caidos, to those who had given their lives in the Spanish Civil War. The distant mountains, with a girdle of mist, added extra poignancy.

I stood and thought about the sacrifices that so many had made less than seventy years ago.

Down a steep hill, up a steep hill: then a long flat sandy stony trail through the pine woods, with the tangy aroma of the pines pervading every step.

No, it wasn't nice and shady: the trail was fully 50 metres wide, and shade did not exist.

The Gloucester Girls and Francesc caught me up ('Hel-**lo**!' beamed Francesc): I walked with them for a while.

It was a hot 14 km to San Juan de Ortega.

The huge, recently restored monastery, designed by San Juan de Ortega himself who had been one of the most famous architects of his era, dominated the bleak hilltop plateau. There were a few dilapidated houses nearby. At more than 4,000 ft (1250 m) it must have been bitter in mid-winter (and I'm sure it still is!), as was most of the Camino.

I was cautiously aware of the cryptic sentences in one of my three Guide Books concerning the Refuge: 'Consistently reported as unhygienic. Own food advised.' Fortunately, the attached restaurant got a good write-up.

Shamak, the Polish film director based in Berlin, was there. He'd had bad leg problems, collapsed on the Camino with a seized muscle, and an Italian lady doctor pilgrim who just happened to be passing with a full medical kit (as you do) administered a quick injection after which he'd been helped down to Villafranca Montes de Oca whence he had limped today.

But he expected to be OK tomorrow.

He told me that Popeye's friend, who sleeps outside (you

haven't met him yet), was pleased with the long flat trail from Villafranca because he'd had to sleep pointing downhill for the previous two days, and now he's got the prospect of a good night's sleep.

The Lady Spoon Player was there, as were the Swedish couple, The English Family On A Walking Holiday, Renata, Maggie and her young Spanish friend, the Gloucester Girls with their tame Francesc, and the English Roses.

So was the Former French Ballet Dancer Now Living In Germany, looking impossibly elegant in a rakish straw hat (mine looks as if it had been sat upon – often, and regularly), an off the shoulder top and wide legged flowing trousers in bright yellow.

She was an incongruous sight on the Camino: how she presented this cool elegance, I just don't know. Sweat, one felt, would never dare to sully her brow.

I washed a few clothes. We had to use the fountains round the side of the monastery, so the washing lines beside the car park (vast!) were generally pretty empty.

The dormitories were basic: by mid-afternoon they reverberated with snoring pilgrims.

Showers were cold. Pilgrims, we are told, have to make sacrifices. I made a sacrifice and did without a shower.

Renata had told me that she'd heard that, after ten days on the Camino, you become increasingly private: and I was finding myself thinking more and more about those early pilgrims who had endured unimaginable hardships for their Faith.

Many were sick before they started: half died before they could return home, from sickness, bandits or attacks by animals. And they couldn't catch a plane back to Pamplona, or a bus to Madrid, when they'd reached Santiago de Compostela. They had to turn round, and walk back home again. Nor could they stop after a week and get a taxi home, to spend another week on the Camino next year and complete the journey over a five year period.

But I won't bore you with my thoughts: this is well documented elsewhere and makes fascinating reading.

Suffice to say that, had it not been for the pilgrims, the Camino and the towns and villages along the way would not now exist. The one had been dependant on the other, and we would all have been the poorer without this.

Car loads of pilgrims were setting off for Burgos from outside the Monastery, once they had got their Pilgrim Passport stamped, their pilgrimage for the year ended.

A German group was accompanied by a large rotund butcher in a car, the husband of one of the pilgrims, who had brought a huge supply of home made (dry) sausages with him and which he distributed to hungry pilgrims along the way.

These were, he said, from the **south** of Germany: far superior (I write without knowledge or comment) to those from the north.

A fellow pilgrim cut off a couple of slabs for me with his knife: both tasted good.

I went to Mass, but thanks to my limited knowledge of Spanish missed the tour behind the scenes and the **free** garlic soup to which the Priest had entertained the congregation.

I wondered where everybody had got to: no wonder the bar was empty.

The soup was very good, they told me: that **really** made me feel better.

The bar had a pilgrim food monopoly for miles around.

I sat with the English Family On A Walking Holiday, father, mother, and children aged 12, 14 and 16, who came from

Crawley barely eight miles from me. They also were going all the way to Santiago de Compostela.

Day 14
San Juan de Ortega to Burgos
25 km   501 km to go

It was August 1, and I was away at first light, about 06.30.

First light was getting later now.

The first few kilometres were along pleasant woodland tracks, then we dropped down to Agés. I resisted the temptation to ask for Rock of Agés, principally because there was nobody about who might understand: the English Family On A Walking Holiday, with whom I'd sauntered through the woods, had strode far ahead by now.

Along the main road, just out of Ages, I met a Spanish pilgrim coming out of the woods. I averted my gaze: I naturally assumed that he'd been obeying a call of nature, and didn't want to appear intrusive. But no!

He'd been crossing a small stone bridge, which he informed me had been built by San Juan de Ortega: and as further invaluable information, he added that he was the Patron Saint of **Technical Architects**, as opposed to Santo Domingo (de la Calzada, of course), who was the Patron Saint of **Architects**.

But both these, he conceded, only applied in Spain: they were not worldwide honours. I could take a small loop, he told me, which joined the main road only a hundred metres ahead: and with that, he continued on his way.

I followed, quite happy that I was able to resist the temptation to cross the bridge.

The Spaniard turned.

'Are you tired?' he asked irritably. No, I wasn't, I said: and as

I couldn't think of any valid reason not to cross the bridge, I did so and took a couple of photographs into the bargain.

This appeared to mollify him. He was a tall, austere aristocratic man, possibly a Technical Architect, and it seemed unwise to upset him.

Through Atapuerca and the mandatory café con leche grande and a cheese bocadillo (you see how easily I am slipping into the language).

Atapuerca is the newly discovered home of the most ancient people in Europe, the fossilised 'Atapuerca Man', which should do wonders for the local tourist trade.

Everywhere there are signs inviting us to various exhibits: and towering over the entrance to the village is an imposing sign to this effect, topped with a painting of (I guess) Atapuerca Man, which looked surprisingly like John Prescott.

My Guide Book omitted to mention any sort of climb out of the village.

Well, it lent a new meaning to the phrase 'stony track'.

I even photographed it when, after a 2 km climb, I crawled over the edge of the quarry to reach the Cross at the summit and got my first view for thirty five years of the industrial city of Burgos. It had changed quite a bit in the intervening years.

Atapuerca Man must have been made of stern stuff: no wonder he was a survivor, pounding these tracks and trails without the benefit of Compeed or orthopaedic sandals.

I descended the steep stony track, bordered by banks of heather and aromatic herbs, to Orbaneja.

Orbaneja is dismissed with the words 'Cross Motorway'. It doesn't come close to describing the industrial desolation which signals the approach to Burgos.

There were two possible routes: I opted for the Circular Route around the Military Installation, which was largely derelict wasteland after the first kilometre of cornfield, rather than the Main Road and getting a bus or taxi as Maggie did.

I fell out onto the main road in Villafría, where I caught up with the voluptuous Anita and her German Friend, looking lost.

Two bars within 50 m! Too good to be true!

Both were shut. It was a holiday.

Well, I've never heard of a bar being shut for a holiday, but the Spanish are obviously made of sterner stuff.

Fortunately, 100 m down the road we found a bar/restaurant that had been able to resist this temptation. I drank... and drank... and drank (water, of course).

Anita and her German Friend set off ahead, along the road: I followed the Camino signs, sometimes with a little light guesswork, crossing major roads with care (as the Guidebook instructed), through miles of housing estates and industrial complexes and finally up a flight of steps to a bridge and then – all the signs disappeared!

My Guide Book instructed me to cross the road and descend steps to follow a complicated route past various sports grounds and the football stadium (bit rough, trudging along with a rucksack on your back, if Burgos F.C. happened to be at home that day).

But – nothing.

A sort of arrow led me down the bridge to the left, where the Council were busy watering the bedding scheme and most of the passers-by outside the park.

I was about to turn back when a lady enthusiastically called over to me: 'No, no, this way is the shady way to the Albergue'.

I didn't care if it turned out to be the non-kosher route: I wasn't going back to do it again now!

I crossed the river by a little footbridge, then followed a paved pedestrian way beneath and between the trees, increasingly urbanised on the far side of the parkland.

Elderly Spaniards strolled slowly along: runners ran: young mothers strolled with pushchairs full of sleeping children: middle aged ladies took their constitutionals; business men ate their sandwiches: rheumy eyed pensioners sat clutching their sticks on the frequent benches.

I asked every second or third person (and there were hundreds of them, but I didn't want to go wrong **now**) if this was the way to the Refuge.

'Si, directo!' and they gestured ahead.

Surely, even I can't lose my way on a straight road when you have to make a really positive effort to leave it!

5 km was the original distance suggested: after 5 km, it was reduced to 3 km, or even 2 km, and one elderly gentleman, eager to show off his knowledge of French, suggested 300 m.

It was actually a further 1.5 km: but he obviously didn't want to upset or disappoint me. When I looked round after about 400m, he'd disappeared.

So, after 8 km on the cool shady riverside walk, I found the Refuge in a beautiful park surrounding the University.

On the stone wall around the park, I found my first yellow arrow *(flecha)* for 2.5 hours. Three arrows close together, to be precise: and all pointing towards the Refuge building which by now could be clearly seen.

There was a further arrow on the fence beside the gate, just in case you were in any doubt.

It was crowded, it was full: and there were lots of toilets and cold showers and a long sort of gently sloping gutter into which nozzles seeped water and in which you could wash your clothes.

You soon realised that the bloke at the top of the sloping gutter got first use of the water: everybody further down got an increasing amount of soap and dirt.

But nobody really objected: they just queued patiently for first use of the water, or surreptitiously rinsed their smalls in the washbasins in the toilets as they usually did.

Shamak was there, looking as urbane as ever, and recounting stories of his feet.

Popeye arrived: a brief greeting, then he was off into the tree spangled parkland with his juggling batons and didgeridoo, probably to brush up his act before León.

He had soon collected a group of eager acolytes.

I soaked my feet in a washing up bowl, and was inspected by the First Aid Man In Residence, who tipped half a packet of salt into the water and told me that I was fine.

He looked like the sort of man you could trust: glasses, clean shaven, a white shirt and impeccable shorts with a razor sharp crease.

My feet felt magical after an hour: I returned the bowl to the vegetable rack, and went off with Anita to find the nearby Supermarket to buy tomorrow's breakfast.

Then I strolled along to the restaurant near the University entrance against which Shamak had specifically warned me.

He was right.

Sister Agatha's lay relation was in charge. She lumped a group of assorted pilgrims together at one table: and a Non-Smoking Trappist Waitress (she had obviously taken a vow of silence) shot into view.

Our order was despatched quickly: she threw mats, serviettes and cutlery into place with unerring accuracy.

We were in, we'd eaten our lukewarm macaroni, and well greased bacon and eggs which slid smoothly across the plate when tilted, mopped up with yesterday's bread, plus a tub of ice cream and (on the positive side) a previously unopened bottle of red wine with a sharp taste, and were out within forty minutes.

We hadn't even had time to introduce ourselves.

We unanimously awarded it a Michelin Black Star.

Shall I name it? No, it wouldn't be fair: and anyway, they might sue me!

OK, I'll take a chance: it was the … no, I'd better not!

Pilgrims, I guess, are just not as popular in big industrial cities as they are in the villages.

6

The Sunbaked Meseta

Day 15
Burgos to Hornillos del Camino
21 km   476 km to go

Shamak and his mates left at 04.00: another group at 05.00. I set out an hour and a half later: crossed the road, and wandered down a shady track through Villabilla to Tardajos. What a contrast leaving Burgos! Virtually no signs guiding you **towards** the Refuge: loads leading you out of town!

I ate my jam and butter bocadillo at Tardajos: I'd found out (it took me a fortnight to do so, I'm a slow learner) that you could buy those little plastic containers of jam that you find on hotel breakfast tables in England, where you can never find one containing marmalade, in the supermarkets.

You spread these on your bread with the plastic 'things' that they supply for you to stir your coffee in fastfood restaurants (I kept a couple in my bumbag).

Don't be tempted to use your penknife, or the jam gets right up into the workings!

Bananas (take care to ask for 'yellow' *amarillo* ones, or they'll palm you off with the green ones) make a sumptuous

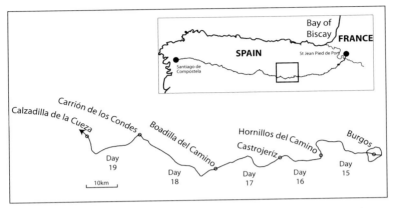

mid-morning snack, topped up with café con leche grande or water straight out of the fountain. And, yes, most of it is drinkable. If it looks suspicious, don't drink: lots of the really dodgy fountains are labelled '*no potable*' (not for drinking).

OK, lesson over: let's get on with walking the Camino.

It was very different for the next 10 km to Hornillos del Camino.

We had reached the *meseta*, the flat wheat growing lands of north west Spain: and for a week or more (160 km), the straight road stretched ahead, with little shade and often with no turning for miles.

2000 ft up, it was bleak in winter, lush and green in spring, and an almost unbearably hot dustbowl in summer.

Some find it tedious: others, as I did, found it hauntingly beautiful with the undulating vastness stretching into the distance on every side and only the sounds of wind, grass and birdsong to break the silence.

Many pilgrims left the Camino at Burgos and hopped on a bus or train to León, the far side of the *meseta*: and after León would come thirty or more kilometres of the even more barren and desolate heathland, the *páramo*.

I toiled up hill for 7 km between the shorn wheat fields, which shimmered in the mid morning heat, as I approached the crest of the *meseta*. Spanish and German cyclists toiled past.

At last, a view of Hornillos del Camino below, basking sleepily amidst a sea of wheat and backed by a forbidding climb to start the next day.

It was a nice little Refuge: 36 beds, one toilet and two showers which surpassed everything that had gone before for sheer inefficiency.

You were lucky to be assailed with enough water to wet your feet. I took twenty minutes to have a cold shave (the first for five days) with my clogged triple blade razor and a bar of carbolic soap.

The blister on my foot was open, raw and bleeding.

Everybody was, as usual, sitting outside in the shade gloomily examining their own and everybody else's feet.

A Spanish lady told me that she had just the thing: an iodine derived compound, marked 'Use before March 2000' (in Spanish, of course!), after which I was to sit with my foot up in the sun.

I didn't fancy the 'in the sun' bit, but I did keep it up and dry, then applied two coats of 'Second Skin' and awaited the next day with trepidation.

I might have a high priced Pilgrims Dinner first, though: €8.50, over £5!

Maggie had already arrived, although without Pedro, whose knee had recovered and he'd left with the 04.00 group. She's amazing: she's tiny, with her back covered with sores from her rucksack straps, little flat feet turned out sideways, and she outwalks us all for speed and distance.

The English Family On A Walking Holiday arrived a little later. They'd given up on the unequal struggle to find the Refuge in Burgos, and gone to a modest hotel from which they'd departed at 09.30 and got thoroughly dehydrated as a result.

The Gloucester Girls with their tame Francesc had left the Refuge at about the same time (no belligerent Nuns to throw out pilgrims there, it was a 'Stay as long as you like' sort of Refuge, with all night music and drinks parties going on in the surrounding parkland).

They looked a bit roasted when they arrived.

By then I was already in the bad books of the Hospitalero.

As a very early (11.30) arrival, with lots of choices of bunks, I'd already changed from upstairs (where I'd swapped mattresses, but without her knowledge) to the cooler downstairs, left my shoes **on** in the dormitory, and then sat down with my foot on the bite valve of my Camelback so that I was surrounded by a large pool of water which she angrily mopped up whilst complaining vigorously about me to a large Spanish audience.

As I didn't understand a word, it didn't particularly bother me. I always prefer people to make remarks about me behind my back, so that it doesn't upset me, and this came under a comparable heading.

Soon the audience were looking at me reproachfully, as they would a wife beater or puppy abuser, so I limped painfully away.

A Japanese pilgrim also tried to change bunks.

Sister Agatha's sister said 'No! Stay!'

And he did. But I didn't blame him for trying: everybody who went out to the yard to peg up their washing covered his face, as he lay on his bunk, with the long curtain that kept out the sun, and they did the same on the way back.

Don't know why he didn't change ends, thinking about it: but it's all water over the bridge now!

I try not to write my diary retrospectively. Pete McCarthy (McCarthy's Bar) told me once (well, I was at a book signing, nothing more closely personal than **that)** to write everything down as it happens.

Well, Pete, that's really good advice, but when you're slogging up a 5 km long rocky trail, an enormous load on your back, sweat streaming down your face and soaking your shirt, it's hard to put into practice: and as a result I've lost many a finely honed epigram that I'd been rehearsing for miles just because sweat running down my arm would soak my notebook.

Just thought I'd mention it.

By Day 15, I thought I'd better make an effort to increase my working knowledge of Spanish. So I added 'food – comida' (or 'alimentación' if you want a word that rolls off the tongue), and 'tienda – shop'. And don't forget 'bebida – drink'.

And Coca Cola, and Fanta… oh, you know those already.

I was already pretty good at *supermercado* – supermarket'.

What's the Spanish for 'sell'? 'Alquilar'? No, it's not, you fool: 'alquilar' means 'rent' or 'hire', and who wants to 'rent' food? It's 'vender'.

'Tiene vender? … Do you sell?' See, I'm almost fluent already.

So we're set for a shopping spree without just relying on *'supermercado*?', inflection rising on the final two syllables and a raise of the eyebrows.

It was Saturday night: the bars beside the square bordering the Refuge were obviously the social centre of the town. The party didn't start until after 10.00pm, with the town fortified by a nourishing meal. It was pleasant to hear the children enjoying themselves as we tried to sleep: their excited shrieks brought sharp responses from their parents, who could shout even louder, and music and song soon began as the town got into the swing of an evening Fiesta.

Fortunately, the next day was Sunday and so there was no

need for them to prepare for work the next day.

The party reached it's peak around midnight: by 02.00, it was almost over.

I missed a little of it: I must have dropped off to sleep.

Day 16
Hornillos del Camino to Castrojeríz
19 km   455 km to go

It's a golden rule of the Camino, that if you descend **into** a town, you have to climb **out** of it, so I get a sinking feeling whenever the road drops sharply down into a town that I'd been targeting for hours.

Well, Hornillos del Camino was no different to the rest.

Six o'clock start, leisurely stroll for half a mile, then straight into a hill: a biggy!

2 km, going up and up a meandering rocky trail: and at the top, an unending plateau.

No sign of habitation at all: just miles and miles of close cropped wheat fields.

Even the few houses that you pass are derelict. Then, just when you've given up all hope of ever seeing another human being, the church and village of Hontanas appears below.

You've walked 11 km in complete solitude: now it's only ½ km down to the little village and **the bar.**

Now, most guide books are pretty non-committal about bars along the way: but two of mine were unanimous in their opinions of this one!

One was slightly more flattering than the other ... 'a small greasy bar offering cheap meals and beds (the scrupulous should stay away)'

The other was more succinct: ... 'a persuasive owner ... who provides copious food cheaply. Women, especially those travelling alone, are strongly advised to stay in the town hall Refuge and avoid this bar'.

Well, of course, I went in. The Gloucester Girls were there, with their tame Francesc.

So were the English Family On A Walking Holiday.

A small aggressive dog was wandering around looking for scraps.

It looked like a set from an art-house Quixote movie: nothing, surely, could be more dark, dingy and, well … indescribably dirty.

I'd ordered my usual café con leche grande before I realised that I'd broken my promise to myself to buy **nothing** there that was not sealed, tinned or with a skin.

The rotund landlord (you had to look closely to be sure whether he was standing up or lying down, he was as near spherical as a man can be) reached a glass from the greasy sink, washed it out with his stubby grubby fingers, wiped it with an even grubbier grey cloth (I'll give you a clue, it had probably started out as a yellow duster), inspected it against the light then rinsed it under the tap.

So that, I reckoned, was pretty OK: well, on a scale of 1 to 5, about 2.

I compensated by ordering an orange.

The Gloucester Girls had survived the encounter, probably protected by the presence of Francesc with his bandaged knees.

I walked past The Swimming Pool Bar, which opened at 08.00. It was now 09.00, and there was no sign of life. Of course, it was a Sunday: but I was quite pleased to find it closed, because it proved that we had been right to go to the bar back up the hill.

They hadn't filled up the swimming pool yet, either: perhaps it wouldn't be open until 11.00 today.

It was a nice 5 km stroll along the hillside, far above the alternative tree shaded road which Alison Raju's book suggested I could follow: but having incurred an enormous guilt complex by taking the **road** from St Jean Pied de Port to Roncesvalles rather than the mountain route on that first day, I didn't want to make things even worse.

The rocky trail descended to the Hospital San Anton, founded by the Antonins, a French Religious Order believed to possess the power of healing St Anthony's Fire (ergotism), a gruesome disease which eventually led to gangrene in fingers and toes because it constricted the veins and cut off the blood supply.

It was ravaging Europe during the 10th century and, fortunately, burnt itself out. Pilgrims came here in search of a cure and were sent on their way after receiving a Blessing with the 'Tau' (a T shaped cross – surely a contradiction in terms, if we're being picky?)

But just to be on the safe side, the monks used to place bread for the pilgrims **outside**, in a niche beside the road.

Pity they didn't know what we know now: that ergot is a fungus that grows on rye, particularly in wet weather, with the fruiting bodies looking remarkably similar to grain. There was an outbreak in Europe a few years ago.

Another effect of ergot was to cause hallucinations.

So now you know: don't say I never teach you anything. Just be careful eating home made rye bread bought from a three fingered baker with a limp after a wet summer, though. No, forget I said that: don't want to be accused of being alarmist.

But, like many dangerous plant-based chemicals, it has a medical use and is now used by doctors as an abortifacient.

Should I buy a Tau, I wondered? No, it was the new **firm** me. What could I do with it if I bought one? Show it to people when I got home, who'd say 'Oh, that's nice'.

So I put a donation into the box, ate one of their boiled sweets, and photographed the ruins and the niches beside the road.

By the way, Alison, these are on the **right** of the road, not the **left**: but as was quite reasonably pointed out to me, it really all depended from which direction you were approaching.

A nice 3 km stroll along the tree lined road to Castrojeríz followed.

Now, Castrojeríz is obviously aligned with Burgos in one important respect: they don't appear to want pilgrims to find out where the Municipal Refuge is hidden.

I teamed up with the English Family On A Walking Holiday, who were just beginning their second lap of this incredibly long town, which rose steeply on either side of the main thoroughfare.

You wouldn't think that it could take almost half an hour to walk through a town of less than 1,500 people!

We gradually narrowed down the whereabouts of the Refuge, almost 200 steep steps above the main road.

A dozen people had already solved the clues by 12.30 and were queuing in an orderly English fashion, led by the Gloucester Girls (and Francesc, of course).

The Refuge didn't open until 14.00: the patio where we waited had been cunningly designed to ensure that it had no shade at all.

There were only 20 bunks advertised. We were numbers 12 to 17 in the queue, so theoretically we were alright.

Maggie had reserved her place by hanging a loaf of bread in a polythene bag from the railings.

A Spaniard dropped his trekking pole over the edge. We watched it somersaulting down beside the steps. Nobody laughed: it might have been one of us.

Another Spaniard arrived and recognized a friend near the

front of the queue. I was now back to 18. By the time the doors opened, I wasn't even in the team.

But we needn't have worried. There were lots of mattresses on the floor: we got about sixty walking pilgrims in before the Completo (full) notice appeared on the door and directed late cyclists to a Refuge down the hill which opened at 3 pm. The Campsite Refuge, far away in the hills (I'd almost got there on one of my early circuits round the town), didn't open until 4 pm.

A huge storm began to build up over the distant hills. Would my washing dry?

I'd already found out that I'd left one of my only two shirts at Hornillos. Should I go back for it? No!

Andrew, the father in the English Family On A Walking Holiday, lent me a T shirt. We stood and watched the lightning amidst the black billowing clouds from the patio, a few heavy raindrops spattering the paving, before we went for a meal together.

Where was the nearest restaurant?

Two hundred metres, we were told. A Spanish two hundred metres: they really don't like to upset you. The English Family On A Walking Holiday, and myself, spread out to look for the missing restaurant. Elderly ladies sitting outside their doors to 'take the air' mobilised their husbands and neighbours to search: their support was enthusiastic and vocal, but unfortunately we didn't understand a word of it, our total Spanish vocabulary was probably less than a hundred words, and that was only valid if they spoke slowly and used hand signals. In the end, we made massive detours to avoid our more enthusiastic helpers and settled on the bar/restaurant opposite a derelict building site that we'd rejected in the first place.

At the back of the tiny bar was a dark cavernous room, packed with pilgrims: the Gloucester Girls and Francesc waved in welcome.

Greasy macaroni, followed by thin steak and chips swimming in oil, staved off the pangs of hunger and induced a strange feeling of malaise.

But it went away in the end: by next midday, I felt almost normal.

The threatened rain hadn't arrived yet: but the hot wind through the night banged the open shutters constantly and made sleep difficult until it finally dropped at about 03.00.

Two hours later, pilgrims began to jostle, at a creeping pace, for places in the washrooms. Once they got through the washroom door, of course, the usual enthusiastic banging and crashing and the fizz! of taps and the intermittent flush of toilets began. Of course, nobody in the main dormitory could hear this, they fondly imagined when they had entered this porcelain sanctuary. They were convinced that the washrooms were totally soundproofed. But once they got back inside the dormitory, they once again became shadowy figures creeping about the huge room, with the odd muffled curse as they tripped over the mound of a nearby pilgrim who was pretending that he was still asleep. Most of them were so quiet that in the end, the silence kept you awake as you strained your ears waiting for the next noise.

Rucksacks were heaved onto shoulders, and pilgrims lurched into the walls or grabbed bunks to balance in the dark.

Then a huge sigh of collective relief as the entrance doors swung open, and then shut with a bang!, and the sound of pilgrims clattering down the steps outside and shouting (quietly) to each other so as not to disturb those still 'asleep' inside … that's early morning life on the Camino.

Day 17
Castrojeríz to Boadilla del Camino
18 km   436 km to go

Those pilgrims who had resisted the lure of an early morning start were entertained to a cup of tea or coffee by the management, boosted by some stale bread that I'd found in the depths of my rucksack and which I dipped into my tub of Primula.

The first two kilometres in the cool dawn, along flat stony tracks, were quite invigorating. Every night, I felt tired after the heat and challenge of the day: every morning, I felt full of vigour, eager to get walking, and today was no exception.

Then came the climb above the still sleeping town. Two winding kilometres, steep and stony: I was passed by every pilgrim from the Refuge who hadn't left early.

I felt gradually drained: the greasy macaroni, steak and chips were beginning to sit heavily as I reached the monument on the hilltop that had been my skyline target since dawn. I was back on the sunbaked *meseta*.

After ten kilometres, I reached the compact Ermita de San Nicolás, a 13th century chapel converted into an eight bunk Refuge by the Italian association of the Friends of St James. It was refreshingly cool inside: and they served me a tiny cup, that looked as though it had come from a doll's house, of sweet black coffee. I was so thirsty that I felt like saying 'Give me the jug!' and draining it to the last bitter dregs.

But I stopped myself just in time.

A Spanish kilometre lay ahead to my target, the café/bar at Itero de la Vega: I'd left the Province of Burgos and was now in Palencia.

An hour later I arrived at a bar, which a rotund Spanish gentleman smilingly informed me was shut. Was there another nearby? No, he seemed pleased to tell me, there wasn't: it was closed today.

But another Spaniard on a bicycle was making encouraging gestures: down a sidestreet was a shop doing a roaring trade, tables and chairs hurriedly set out on the pavement, and serving café con leche (fairly grande), soft drinks, honey flavoured Muesli bars, cakes ... I had some of everything.

I invested in a store of Muesli bars for the rest of the day. These melted deep down inside my rucksack, but congealed in the cool of the evening to form a waterproof coating that I could peel off.

I ate some of everything: I was there for an hour.

Lorenz (and his wife) from Majorca, who turned out to be a banker and not a Technical Architect, prevailed on me to stop eight kilometres ahead at Boadilla del Camino rather than continuing a further six kilometres to Frómista.

I drank 1.5 litres of water during these eight kilometres, and still never had a pee: I was basically dehydrated. The track rose steadily for almost six kilometres: there was no shade at all between the golden stubbled wheatfields.

But what a wise decision to stop at Boadilla!

I was so pleased at my decision that I suggested playfully to a pilgrim later that it should be called **Bocadilla** del Camino: after a few minutes of careful explanation, he brightened suddenly and said 'Ah! I see, a play upon words!'

He didn't seem all that amused, though.

I passed the tiny 12 bunk Municipal Refuge with it's bare debris strewn garden.

It opened at 14.00: it was now 12.30.

Round the corner I came upon the fantastic, sumptuous Albergue en el Camino: a privately owned Refuge of surpassing elegance.

Weed free lawns, dotted with containers of flowers, guided

weary travellers to the shaded entrance hall. Edward, the young owner, and his two elegant Canadian acolytes who had completed the Camino in May and returned to help out for the rest of the summer, welcomed me with open arms (figuratively speaking, that is: I was a bit too hot and sweaty to make close physical contact appealing to either party).

August 10th, he told me, was when his season was virtually over: after that, it was downhill to winter.

The shady patio, tables groaning beneath their load of cool drinks and sheltered further by enormous sunshades, was full of the more elderly pilgrims gloomily inspecting their own and each other's feet.

Their conversation was akin to the discussion of bowel movements in the lounges of old people's homes.

I was led through the gardens to the long, single storey dormitory block, bicycles stacked in heaps outside and shoes piled in the lobby: it was a NO SHOES area.

As usual on such occasions, I began to wish that I hadn't rejected my sandals on the grounds of weight and space back home in England.

There was a large shady lounge inside the entrance lobby, furnished in such opulence with comfortable chairs and settees, low tables and ornate mirrors that it looked like a brothel in a Clint Eastwood Western. Those in Gary Cooper Westerns, of course, were much more basic and open, with room for the proprietress to fire warning shots amidst the punters from a balcony above an impressively wide staircase.

This, added to the superb restaurant, the beautiful gardens and the genuine welcome, made it a place in which to luxuriate.

The unisex toilets were spacious and gleamingly tiled, with the wall above each washbasin festooned with loops of different coloured electric wires protruding from the plaster (fortunately out of reach, so we couldn't succumb to the temptation to test whether or not they were live). Maybe next year they'll have lights fitted to the ends. The only downside was the dark, hot claustrophobic dormitories, with scarcely room to swing a rucksack let alone a lively cat. But what the heck! After all, the only thing you do there is sleep.

I got the lower bunk in the far corner facing the washroom door. The air was very still.

Even so: four stars!

Edward (the same name as your Prince: no, not Charles, he is always hunting and shooting and his nose in the air), worked tirelessly with the Canadian girls and his parents.

His mother, who usually does the cooking, was ill in bed today. I just hoped that it wasn't food poisoning.

The food was good, and the restaurant was packed: two sittings, thirty at each!

I'd heard so much about the spirituality of the Camino: but this was August, holiday month, and the Camino was now awash with young fit cyclists and walkers for whom it had become an athletic Challenge with the guaranteed support of cheap, well spaced Refuges along the way.

The Albergue was by mid-afternoon packed with fit 'athletes' in their early and mid twenties, plus a number of middle aged couples for whom it was a rewarding experience to be savoured year after year with Santiago their spiritual goal. A few more, individuals or in groups, were walking the Camino for deeply spiritual or very personal reasons. They tended to keep themselves to themselves.

In Burgos, for example, I had met a young German, spotty, pasty faced, bespectacled and pony tailed. He confided that the Camino was helping him to overcome his fears, such as losing his way (don't talk to me about **that** one!): he had never been out of a city before, and it was a cathartic experience.

I felt very sorry that I hadn't spared him more time, just to let him talk.

But somehow, in the three weeks of late July and early August, the 'fun' element of the athletic 'challenge' came to the forefront: and why not? It was a modern expression of the reason for the original inception.

I met Ada, a statuesque German lady who spoke faultless English after trekking through most of the world and settling for eighteen months in Australia. The Camino, she told me, was something that she just had to do: she wanted to visit every church along the way and was sad that so many were shut.

I hid my stubbly chin as best I could, as we spoke: my triple blade razor (a major sales point in Sainsburys) was now blocked solid with congealed soap, and cold water shaving was now only an option under extreme circumstances.

She gave me a spare disposable razor that she had with her: hopefully, it had not been used. I pushed such thoughts to the back of my mind, and twenty minutes of pain paid off with a red prickly chin.

I could now escort a lady to dinner and look her in the face. What did we eat?

Oh, spaghetti … and tomato sauce, of course.

Day 18
Boadilla del Camino to Carrión de los Condes
25 km   418 km to go

Surreptitious movement began in the claustrophobic dormitory by 0400: by 0500, all pretence at silence had gone, the washroom door at the foot of my bed was wide open and the lights on inside, boots were being freely worn and by 0530 the entire room was empty apart from myself, Ada and the painfully thin Elisabetha, whose big shy smile lit up every room.

Ada did the unthinkable: SHE TURNED ON THE LIGHTS IN A PILGRIM DORMITORY BEFORE SIX O'CLOCK! And nobody complained: probably because there was nobody else there.

Breakfast at 0600 for us few, and lots of cyclists. Were **they** all doing it for spiritual reasons?

A family of eight, including two young children, occupied the main table. All wore identical yellow Tour de France jerseys and tight blue mid-thigh length cycling shorts.

Mother sat at the head of the table, smoking heavily, and beaming at her family in between intermittent bursts of coughing.

Today would have been a good day to have started **really** early: the four o'clock starters knew a thing or two.

After the first mile of good footing, it was straight down to the footpath along the canal bank. The Canal de Castilla is a hugely important irrigation canal, apparently: for pilgrims, it was great, flat as you like for 3 km.

To be fair, not many canals are hilly: although the feature of the Grand Union Canal from Gas Street Basin in Birmingham to London includes a climb up a 600 ft hill.

True, it takes sixty miles to get to the top and another sixty to get to the bottom on the other side: but it's undeniably a hill.

The whine of approaching mosquitoes, roused from the pools beside the boggy bank by the aroma of cheesy feet (no, I'm not being deliberately sensational, that **is** the attractant for mosquitoes, according to recently published research: that's why you get bitten on the feet, toes and ankles), kept me busy.

I skipped and slapped all the way to the lock, which I crossed and dropped down into the outskirts of Frómista.

Fatigue and the fear of not getting a bed had stopped me pressing on there last night: it had been so easy this morning that I was beginning to torture myself with self doubts. No, wait, that sounds a bit heavy: what I mean is, the thought briefly flitted into my mind. As Lorenz said, there's a long way to go. Listen to your body: and I wouldn't now have a (hopefully) new razor, so it was obviously all for the best.

I zipped into the heavily pilgrim populated bar, after a visit to the Hole In The Wall across the road to boost my funds. They don't accept cards at Refuges or in the tiny café/bars along the Camino: it's not like Majorca!

Now, I don't like to be too – well, basic – but please, check the safety of your toilet if you have any sort of doubts! I was comfortably seated, busy amassing my Pilgrim Insurance for the day ahead from the roll on the wall, when I leaned over just that little bit further and found that the throne was not bolted to the floor. It was freestanding.

I managed to push myself upright, spreadeagled against the wall at about 45 degrees: but it was the sort of nasty moment that could well have ruined any prospect of a good relationship with the owner of the bar.

Almost as soon as I left the bar, I was on to the beautifully graded Senda de Peregrinos, a footpath running parallel to the road and constructed especially for pilgrims and leading all the way for 19 km to Carrión de los Condes.

Well, it didn't lead all the way for me!

Somehow, I lost my way on a straight road (don't worry, I've done the same thing many times before!) and found myself wandering through the little village of Población de Campos. Yes, there had been a little yellow arrow that had drawn me away from the main road: but that, apparently, was directing weary pilgrims to the tiny refuge, rather than vigorous walkers intent on 'getting in the miles'.

Lorenz and his wife were sitting outside a little corner shop, sipping a can of Fanta.

Lorenz was wearing his usual **50th Anniversary of the D Day Landing 1944-1994** T-shirt. I tried to buy some bananas: no luck.

I didn't get back on to the main road: instead (the alternative route), I wandered through Villaviejo and then along the bank of the River Ucieza for 5 km.

I met a lady collecting snails. She already had a carrier bag half full: they seemed healthy and mobile, although some were ungratefully trying to escape. Perhaps they knew something that I didn't.

I guessed that either she didn't get on very well with her neighbours, and was going to throw them over the wall into their garden when they were out, or she was going to eat them. Perhaps it was a special family meal for the in-laws.

The carrier bag advertised a well know chain of supermarkets (no, it wasn't Sainsbury's). It was Merca Centro, if you really want to know: but I guess that you could pack enough snails to feed a family of five into a Sainsbury's bag if you tried.

As I walked along, I saw one that she'd missed.

Should I tell her?

He looked up at me reproachfully and scuttled off into the reeds.

It was baking hot: not a breath of wind stirred the air.

What a place to set up World Record attempts: 100 metres, long jump, triple jump.

The wind gauge would seize up through lack of movement. Mind you, the 100m would have to be a solo attempt: too narrow to get two runners side by side without the outside one falling into the river, but it's probably worth mentioning to the Frómista Town Council. Think what it would do for their tourist trade!

I was getting worried that I might be lost: but I found an arrow which guided me away from the river bank and over a bridge onto a little road and into a village that was so small that it didn't appear even to have a name (but it was probably Villasirga). The heat embraced me like an oppressive blanket: and there were still 6 km to Carrión de los Condes.

I came across a tilted wooden sign with an arrow, fixed to a barn wall. It said 'BAR'.

I was there before you could spell 'BAR': 200 metres in world record time, carrying a rucksack.

Fitzy, an Irishman from Cork, and his friend Santi (from Santiago) were the only other customers. Like me, they were on their way to Carrión.

I suggested that it would make a good title for yet another Carry On film (Carry on to Las Condes: Carrión? Get it?) Santi was interested in the concept: 'What is Carry On?'

'Oh, they are amusing pornographic films' said Fitzy. Personally, I thought that this was a little harsh, but I couldn't think of a better definition on the spur of the moment.

Santi looked blank: I left Fitzy trying to explain in Spanish with an Irish accent.

I think he was on a loser: Santi kept coming back with 'But why should they want to make a pornographic film in Carrión de los Condes?'

Best to get out quickly, I thought: a can of Fanta and two bottles of water later, I was on my way along the Senda de Peregrinos, which I had rejoined by accident.

I tried to edge closer to the main road because whenever a big lorry passed, the wind ruffled my hair.

I even put on my battered straw hat: this made my head even hotter.

I had to speed up: I was playing the numbers game again, and yet I was still stopping to take photographs (meaningful ones, of course).

Fitzy and Santi strode past: Santi was saying 'But why do this in Carrión …?'

Fitzy looked stressed: his lips tightened a little as he glanced across at me.

Carrión de los Condes is now a quiet little town: but it had once had 12,000 inhabitants and is reputed to have been a town where the Moorish overlords had required the Christians to surrender 100 Virgins every year.

Happily, this requirement (if it ever existed) lapsed many centuries ago.

Now, the town is only a quarter of that original size.

There are two Refuges there: and I missed them both by three places. Not even room for a sleeping mat on the floor.

The English Family on a Walking Holiday, the Gloucester Girls (and Francesc), Ada and Maggie all looked sorrowful: but **that** wasn't going to get me a bed!

It was, after all, 1.39: I'd started off late and even had several breakfasts, and I guess the cyclists had got in first.

The Hospitalero was pretty fair about it: the main square was littered with cyclists, and if you didn't arrive by 12.30 then I guess the places were up for grabs.

She took pity on me, creaked her way to the door, and pointed out the way across the square to the Hostal Santiago, one stage up from a Refuge, where you had beds with blankets provided.

I spoke into the voice box beside the door, trying to sound like just the sort of guest that the Hostal was trying to attract.

The Concierge let me in, and took me upstairs for an

interview in Spanish.

I recognised the odd word.

Five sharing a room? €11 each? Shower/toilet/washbasin for the sole use of the Famous Five?

It sounded like Paradise. I wiped the sweat from my brow with the remnants of my Saharan towel that hung from my rucksack bungies.

She obviously saw me as a deserving cause: she gave me a can of beer, free, in a unique gesture.

Elisabetha (no, not the one from Boadilla, another one) and her boyfriend were occupying the two beds by the window. I got the one by the toilet door. The Birmingham Two soon arrived to claim the middle ground.

Elisabetha was walking the Camino because it was just something that she had to do: she'd give up her job in a cosmetics factory and wanted to work as a volunteer in Africa. Now that's the sort of person for whom the Camino fills a real purpose!

I did my washing: it had to be hung from the balcony rails, two floors above the street, and I was dependant on the vice like grip of my Spar pegs to keep me clothed next morning.

They did! I'll go to Spar again!

It was better than the Refuge: they had absolutely nowhere to hang their clothes to dry there.

Mind you, it might not have worked out quite so well for we Hostal washers.

Through an unopenable window halfway up (or down, depending which way you were going) the stairs, I saw a pair of voluminous white knickers and a solitary red peg lying on the asbestos roof below.

They would lie there for ever, I guessed, as mute testimony, unless a large knickerless lady daringly hooked them up from far above in a moment of extreme desperation.

Ada had suggested that we might meet for a meal.

We wandered along looking for a restaurant that looked like the sort of place that we'd like to visit: unfortunately, I made the mistake of walking into the kitchen rather than sidestepping the wall into the dining room. I made a mental note to order food requiring a minimum of preparation.

Over our cosy spaghetti and tomato sauce, she confessed that she, like so many pilgrims, was 'spiritual'.

Did I know a town called Bath in England? Yes, I said, they had been the champion rugby club in England for many years. She didn't seem over impressed by the information. She looked a little blank, even though she lived near Heidelburg which had occupied a similar place in German rugby.

Anyway, she continued, it had been revealed to her that in one of her four or five previous lives, she had been Headmistress of a Girls School in Bath in 1899.

Did I know which school this might be? No, this was a little outside my scope of interests: and although she suggested that we might go and continue this stimulating discussion elsewhere, I thought it best to get back to the Hostal to prepare for tomorrow.

I was in my room by 9.00 pm: lights were already out, shades were down, and Elisabetha and her boyfriend, and the female section of the Birmingham Two, were already in bed and asleep.

The washing was dry, and, equally important, still there. I decided to postpone packing until the morning. My usual mistake.

Day 19 dawned early: 1.42, to be precise. I was roused by raucous laughter and traditional Spanish music, both at maximum decibels, from the bar across the street.

At 2.00, one of the customers tried to leave, but his car was difficult to start. He tried, I'll give him that: my, how he tried!

It eventually burst into action: exhaust problems were evident, judging by the throaty roar. Raucous laughter accompanied it all.

At 2.30, the landlord started to stack tables around his customers, who valiantly tried to keep the party going: but by 3.00 a.m. even they gave up the unequal struggle and their laughter disappeared into the distance.

I had one nasty moment when I thought that they were coming back: but it was a false alarm!

I just hoped that he hadn't alienated his customers by closing early. Somehow, I fell asleep again.

Day 19
Carrión de los Condes to Calzadilla de la Cueza
17 km   393 km to go

The Birmingham Two woke by 0500, vying for toilet space with Elisabetha and her boyfriend.

I was pleased to hear that they'd all had an uninterrupted night's sleep.

They all seemed relieved when I suggested that they put on the light: by 0600, they'd all left.

I had my own room and toilet: I could even have a bath if I wished!

When I sat up in bed, I didn't bang my head on the springs above!

It was magic!

I breakfasted in my room, sitting beside the desk (yes, **desk!**):

orange, banana, bread dipped in Primula, yoghourt. No spoon for my yoghourt: but if you get the thin walled tubs (cheapos) and palpate them (technical word, the thing that doctors do when they squeeze your lumps, don't worry), you can extrude the contents straight into your mouth. Go on, get one out of the fridge and try it: although it's best if you let it warm up in your pocket or handbag for a day first.

It was almost like breakfast at home.

But I made the mistake of thinking that I had too much time. When I left at 0700, it was already getting warm: the old red bricks of the house walls were like storage heaters, making me sweat as I walked past.

I lost my way in the first 100 yards: a man with a wheelbarrow set me on my way.

Over the bridge, then four kilometres of shady road almost uncluttered by cars before I turned onto the red stony footpath between the shade free close cropped wheatfields that stretched, straight as a die, for 12 km to Calzadilla de la Cueza.

It was interrupted only after 4 km by a concrete picnic table area, close to a country road crossed by the Camino, and which was so surrounded by a sea of debris that even weary pilgrims avoided it. There was a tap and stagnant sink there as well.

A group of car-supported pilgrims were adding to the debris, rummaging through the boot looking for more to contribute. Three of them were walking: the other two drove ahead, ready to take their place as walkers next day. So that the walkers wouldn't be overburdened, they took their rucksacks on in the car and met up with them again a few kilometres down the Camino.

I hoped that they wouldn't all stay in the Refuges: but I feared that they would.

Pilgrims by Camion, rather than Camino.

At 11.30, I crested a hill and saw the little village of

Calzadilla de la Cueza below.

The thirty bed Refuge opened at 12.00: I joined the line of pilgrims grabbing what shade they could beside the door.

I was actually number eleven in the queue: surely, those closer to the door couldn't find twenty friends in the next half hour to eject me from 'the team'?

The Gloucester Girls (and Francesc) were already there: Julia had a bad foot, the sole split and septic, but she had only four more days to last as they were returning to England from León leaving Francesc, his knees now free of bandages, to continue to Santiago alone.

It was the first time that I'd been aware of the large imaginative tattoo on Julia's arm: on closer inspection (didn't like to look too closely because... well, it's easy to get a reputation) turned out to be a massive mosquito bite.

The recent nightly storms (and it looks like another tonight) had filled up the stagnant ditches beside the road and the happy mosquitoes were coming out in droves to celebrate with a tasty snack of pilgrim on the hoof.

This looked like being the Mosquito Centre of the Camino: and I'd got the lower bunk by the back door leading to the yard.

By midday, I'd already despatched two with my bare hands in the toilets.

The Refuge has seven (unisex) showers and three toilets: the showers, as ever, unique. Once you get inside, it's straight into the tray: you can't turn the water on from outside, and judge strength and heat. It's all or nothing. The clothes hooks are outside the door, so that you have to get out naked to grab your towel. And no, you can't hang it over the door: as I soon found, it gets wet!

But the showers are HOT: and for the first time for days, I washed my hair. The small packet of shampoo that I'd pocketed at the Hilton last year looked like lasting for three weeks, used sensibly!

The elegant Lady Hospitalero boosted her income by giving massages: her rubbing table was beside her desk in the office, and occupied her full time during the long afternoons, as pilgrims on bicycles swooped down from the hills for a *sello* and a rub down.

Personally, I resisted the temptation: after all, €5 would get me a meal.

I went out and did my washing instead.

The yard looked like a recently cleared demolition site, the high walls topped with broken glass (just like my grandfather's garden in Nottingham sixty years ago).

Was this to keep pilgrims IN, or locals OUT?

The sinks were tucked into a shady corner, cold taps, plastic bowls for individual projects, and a concrete scrubbing board: you all sloshed around companionably, before hanging your clothes up on the miles of drooping nylon line against sunbaked walls.

It was wonderful: what more could any pilgrim want from life?

Well, food comes to mind: and I joined the Gloucester Girls (and Francesc) at a really upmarket restaurant round the corner from the Refuge, a beautiful polished wood bar packed with pilgrims and a dining room with small elegant tables, soft lights, and a rather special range of paper table cloths.

I celebrated passing the halfway mark from St Jean Pied de Port to Santiago de Compostela.

We ate a different meal to the usual: NO PASTA!

There'd obviously been a run on it in the area, so they served up a thick and nourishing potato soup followed by The Englishman's Support Abroad, two fried eggs and chips.

The landlord, like the team at Burgos, had obviously been trained at the No Charm School Of Waitering. He had this same manual dexterity as he threw mats and cutlery unerringly into place, and sighed heavily, hand on hip, as he waited for his bread-and-butter clientele to choose from the hastily scribbled menu.

We walked slowly back along the flattest bit of road that we could find, out of deference to Julia's foot: mine were great, and I was now numbered amongst the ranks of seasoned pilgrims who walked about with a firm stride looking pityingly at the groups of Camino virgins gloomily discussing the state of their feet.

I daubed myself in Deet and went to bed. Great night's sleep: not a single mosquito 'whined and dined'.

The launderette at Calzadilla de la Cueza

7

León – and still on the Meseta!

Day 20
Calzadilla de la Cueza to Sahagún
21 km   376 km to go

We all woke early: I was up by 0515, front of the queue, and sat outside in the glare of the security lights dipping two day old bread into my deteriorating Philadelphia, which slid from side to side of it's plastic container. A blackening banana, some dry digestive biscuits donated by Francesc in Santo Domingo, water from the tap in the back yard, and by 0559 I was **off**!

A few cars and lorries passed, headlights cheering up the dawn, as I strolled along the Senda de Peregrinos (The Pilgrim Trail) beside the main road for 6 km to Ledigos. I even resisted diverting to a roadside bar which looked very neat and welcoming.

Certainly the two pilgrims inside looked happy.

But my schedule dictated non-stop to Terradillos de los Templarios, 10 km from Calzadilla and an almost equal distance to Sahagún, which you could see far ahead along the unbending and increasingly busy road.

Terradillos de los Templarios had a splendid name, and a past

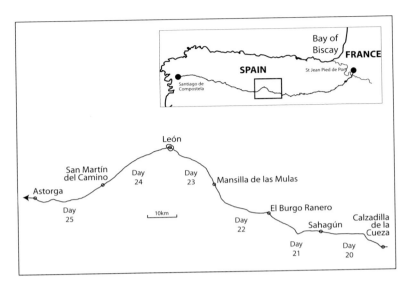

which didn't match it's present. No bar, but the Refuge, beside the Camino through the village, served breakfast now that all the pilgrims from the night before had left.

It looked a real tip: but when you poked your head inside the door, there was a nice cosy shady room with lots of long tables and chairs, and a spotless kitchen where the Hospitalero was beavering about getting €3 breakfasts for us sweaty pilgrims gathered on the patio and the steps.

By 0900 we were into the heat of the day: it was a relief to reach the shady square and drinking fountain at San Nicolás del Real Camino and slump onto a seat against the wall. I sympathised with a squat muscular 'oldie', who was forced to retire hurt ('I have broken my knee'): he climbed into a taxi and was off to Sahagún.

Joanna and her partner were packing their rucksacks beside the fountain, which was doing splendid service for the builders putting up a new house. Real estate seemed to be booming, new

The meseta: take any minute from eight days

houses going up whilst dilapidated cottages tumbled around them.

Joanna was wearing a Ponsonby (Auckland, New Zealand) rugby shirt. I commented that our son Cameron had played for Ponsonby during his 'year out'.

So had she, but ten years after Cameron: in fact, she'd not long got back from New Zealand. She was the Basque and Spanish National Women's XV prop, and had played for Ponsonby for a couple of seasons and then for Nelson.

She looked as if she could have given Jason Leonard a good going-over in the scrum, but she'd been too small to prop regularly in New Zealand and had been playing flanker or No. 8 mostly. I wasn't surprised, I'd seen at first hand the size of some of the Maori girls propping over there.

Her partner, a big guy but dwarfed by the muscular Joanna, had gone over with her for a working holiday. He was commiserating with her now: after a bright start from Burgos, blisters were taking their toll and Sahagún looked like being the end of the road for her this year.

I was soon in the Province of León. The name change didn't make any difference, it was still baking hot: at one point, a breeze started to get up but was obviously tired and decided to lie down again. Now, don't get me wrong: it can't be too hot for me, I hate the cold and the wet, so this is just an observation without comment. But, yes, it **was** hot: **really** hot!

If there was one thing to keep in mind, it was to Keep Hydrated (drink, to the non-scientific reader), and to Protect Yourself Against The Sun. What's that? That's two things? Well, you know what I mean.

Sahagún stood around the top of a hill ahead, the road winding it's way to the crest. I could have gone straight there: but I decided not to cheat, and took the off road roundabout route through the fields, past the little chapel of the Ermita Virgen del Puente onto the Camino Frances de la Virgen, under the flyover, past the station and into the old town.

The Municipal Albergue (the Refuge), high up in the tower of the beautifully restored Trinidad church beside the small square, had room for lots of pilgrims: 64 in eight bunk alcoves in the open plan dormitory, and goodness knows how many on mattresses in the stairwell, and in the auditorium of the theatre leading off the entrance hall.

Joanna, her foot propped up against the wall, and her partner were in the bunks opposite.

Security, roof over your head, sturdy bunk, good kitchen, showers, toilets and somewhere to wash your clothes: not bad for €3 (£2).

Now, let's have a little teach-in about Showers in Refuges.

First thing to notice: if you enter a shower stall and the floor is dry, it's obviously not working. You can get confirmation by looking for dry, dead flies in the corners.

Secondly, sometimes they're working, but the shower head is missing. If you're a Camino Virgin (and you're only a Camino Virgin once), and you haven't looked carefully first, you get a fierce invigorating jet of usually very cold water.

Thirdly, those shower heads on flexes that fit really neatly into slots against the wall and stand firmly upright in England, don't in Refuges. They might have done once, but they don't now. If they do, be suspicious.

This is **a good thing,** because they lie across the taps and you can adjust the temperature of the water (in the unusual event of the hot taps containing anything other than cold water) without inflicting personal pain.

They were wonderfully hot at Sahagún: it was great!

Fourthly, the door rarely locks: but don't worry, after the first three days you've lost all your inhibitions anyway.

In fact, at Arca (so close to Santiago that it didn't matter anyway), there was only a sort of waist high bulkhead inside the doorless shower stall round which the participant walked, and which enabled any would-be showerer to assess instantly

a) whether the shower stall was occupied and

b) if you're that way inclined, the sex of the occupant.

Fifthly (and finally) the hook on which you are invited to hang your clothes is often either **outside** the door (so you have to go out naked to get your towel) or, if inside the shower cubicle, is in direct line of fire in a very narrow space between shower tray and door.

So, if you're showering, put your back against the wall with your naughty bits pointing **outwards**, and direct the jet **inwards**, towards the back wall.

Basically, it's your own fault if you hose down your own clothes.

Sometimes, of course, there is no shower tray: water is

optimistically expected to run down a slight slope into a central grating, which is often blocked (do you **really** fancy clearing it of hair and bits of soap and toilet paper with your own bare hands, or do you leave it to the next occupant?). So water generally bypasses this arrangement, and overflows into the washroom where it soon builds up, often an inch or so deep, and might even creep out beneath the door of the washroom into the fringe of the dormitory.

Often, good spirited pilgrims will get mop and bucket and squeegee it up. But generally, they won't: that's why it's generally a good idea to get a bunk as far away from the washroom door as possible, because the further away from the door you are, the drier the floor becomes. Pilgrims paddle the water into the dormitory anyway.

And presumably, there's less danger of rampant verruca and athlete's foot: although, as your towel generally drags its way along the floor, it's probably immaterial.

I sat in the shade outside the church, sipping a can of Nestea (love it, but can't stand it in England), watching the world go by. It's one of my favourite afternoon occupations. I like to think that I'm quite a deep thinker, a 'street philosopher' at times (you don't believe **that,** surely! It's probably just when I'm hot and tired, and need a rest).

I'd just had a long conversation with a French lady, who'd spoken ever so slowly (in French) and enunciated perfectly so that I could understand just about every word. She also had met the Spanish group in the minibus, who I had met on the way to Calzadilla de la Cueza, and who had kindly given me a peach beside the rubbish dump that passed for a picnic spot.

Yes, she confirmed, they took it in turns to walk and ride, one day off, one day on.

So did a German group, she said: surely not the sausage fancier who I'd met at San Juan de Ortega, distributing The Best of the Wurst. Yes, 'wurst' is German for sausage: pretty neat, eh?

Hardly, she postulated, the spirit of the Camino.

Lots of young cyclists, she continued (like the family group that I'd met at Boadilla), especially in the holiday month from mid-July to mid-August, were using the Camino and the attendant Refuges to support a personal 'challenge': and even 'Powerwalkers' were putting in a week on the Camino, at a steady 6 or 7 km an hour, as a gruelling athletic Challenge.

Would it be too cynical, she continued (I had to slow her down a bit here, she speeded up as she got more excited!) to suggest that for many young people, admittedly 'hooked' on the beauty of the Spanish countryside, the Camino was a cheap well-supported Challenge trail and often at the expense of true pilgrims, who sometimes failed even to get a bed.

Many Refuges, however, shut their doors to cyclists until late in the afternoon, kicked them out early, and refused to open for **any** reason until early afternoon.

She was a bit put out: she'd reached a Refuge at exactly 0800 (throwing out time!) after an early start, and they wouldn't even let her go in for water.

You could see it rankled: her entire measured discourse had probably been leading up to this one specific point.

But I looked round the kitchen and dining area at Sahagún, and saw a sea of middle-aged and elderly faces and a few youngsters for whom, from conversation, I knew that the Camino had a deeper purpose.

Perhaps the French lady had been judging too harshly?

But deep down, I knew that she hadn't: there is a rapidly increasing change of emphasis which can never now be stopped. Things evolve: and whatever the initial intent, every

'Challenger' gained from the Camino and from the people that they met along the way.

That, folks, is evolution in action.

A family of serial photographers were in action beside the imposing statue of St James outside the front door: mother, father, young son.

Father photographed mother and son, then mother alone, then son, in two poses: standing self-consciously, and embracing the giant statue. Mother did the same for father and son: son also was pressed into service. Did they want me to photograph the three together, to complete the set? Yes please, they beamed. I thought that, as it was so popular, I might as well have one of myself; especially as the Serial Photographers were all by now pretty expert. Just to be on the safe side, I took one or two of St James by himself.

It's amazing how you can entertain yourself for hours along the Camino: the Serial Photographers (I'd thought at first that they were Japanese with Mediterranean complexions) now had the capacity to bore their family (and friends) for months, and they probably repeated the procedure all the way to – wait, they were probably only there as tourists for the afternoon, so why not remember the day?

I wandered through the town, down the steep narrow roads, past the cafés with packed pavement tables. I joined them, and toyed with a café con leche grande and a Magnum (the ice cream, not the gun). Then I bought a few postcards because the pictures are photographs better than any I could take. I'll probably cut the wording off the bottom, put them in my Camino photograph album, and pretend I took them myself.

No, I won't: oh well, perhaps I will…

I strolled along to a Hole in the Wall to draw out €150. The message flashed up that it only had €20 notes: please could I choose a sum that matched what they had in stock?

I felt hungry: I went into a cake shop, with a restaurant at the back, for a Pilgrim Meal *(Menu de peregrinos, por favor?)*. It was €6.60, but they **did** serve a good class boiled sweet with the coffee afterwards. The girl behind the counter was busy: she doubled as shop assistant and waitress.

The menu was translated into English, French and German, and was slightly dog-eared, so it was obviously not chef's off the cuff, spur-of-the-moment dishes.

I liked the sound of Tubular Powders: turned out to be macaroni, but I'll forever now think of Macaroni Cheese as Tubular Powders.

Three multi lingual German Mothers (teachers all) helped me with the negotiations: they were returning to the Camino in an all out attempt to reach Santiago in their summer holidays, after having completed the section to Burgos the previous spring in cool sunny weather which had made it such a pleasure to walk between flower filled fields, and with ample space in the Refuges even at 5 pm in the afternoon.

This was a rude awakening for them.

They had started from Frómista that day, walked to Carrión, caught a bus and then walked the final 13 km to Sahagún between 4.00 pm and 6.00 pm in searing 100ºF heat.

Their reward was three mattresses in the theatre auditorium: and they were lucky to get those!

Now, I've mentioned before that there were signs of an outbreak of red hair amongst Spanish ladies along the Camino: and in Sahagún, it's become almost an epidemic.

Dark red hair, fighting a losing battle with the lustrous black hair of the traditional Spanish beauty, and unnaturally white teeth, bleached like Dieter's tombstones, can be a nasty shock coming at you out of the gloom of the Town Hall.

The Refuge was hot tonight!

Built into the top of the tower, there were no windows to open, and the noisy ventilation system (such as it was) was switched off at night to avoid keeping pilgrims awake.

Day 21
Sahagún to El Burgo Ranero
18 km   355 km to go

The temperature soared into the 100sF: we sweated through the long night (long? Action began by 04.00).

Me? I'd thought that, if I leapt nimbly from my bunk at 05.30, I'd make the 06.00 start well ahead of the pack and do the 18 km to El Burgo Ranero before the heat of the day.

Now 18 km doesn't seem very long: but pilgrims spend hours agonising about where to stop the next evening, and it's all based on the distance to the next Refuge.

I had the choice between 5 km to Calzada del Coto, 13 to Bercianos de Real Camino, 18 to El Burgo Ranero, 31 to Reliegos, 38 to Mansilla de las Mulas and 57 to León! A very hot day, loads of water to carry and a heavy rucksack (12 kg! Don't know how some pilgrims get the weight down to 7 or 8!) : I chose El Burgo Ranero, next day Mansilla de las Mulas, and day after, León. I'd have liked a further 15 km or so over these three days: but over a walk of five to six weeks, what the heck! There's harder days with longer distances to come!

Half the 64 bunks were empty by 05.30: Francesc was wolfing down his second mug full of chocolate chip cornflakes and milk, and the Gloucester Girls were showing signs of impatience. Joanna just snorted, and gave her battered feet a

Breakfast at Sahagún

little more elevation: her partner was preparing to go it alone.

All around was the insistent sound of pilgrims brushing their teeth with battery powered toothbrushes.

I made the mistake of switching on the ventilation system and extractor fans in the toilets and washrooms.

By the time I'd got myself sorted, and out into the cyclist filled square that looked like one of the CTC (Cyclists Touring Club) outings of my youth, it was 06.30, and I knew, I knew, I'd done it **again**!

I crossed the bridge over the tree lined river Cea. The story goes that when the Moors and Christians were fighting for control of northern Spain, an exhausted Christian army camped near Sahagún and (for some strange reason) stuck their lances into the ground. Next morning they awoke, and found that their lances had sprouted roots, branches and leaves; which must not only have left them rather surprised, but presumably made them ineffective as a fighting force.

Who won next day? Don't know.

Did they thrash the Moors about the head with leafy

branches?

Anyway, it was good walking for 6 km to Calzada del Coto. Then, choices!

Did I take the Calzada de los Peregrinos, or the Real Camino Francés?

I'll tell you what the guide book said, and leave you to guess which route I took:

Calzada de los Peregrinos

… an old Roman road … very isolated and … little or no water, no accommodation, no shops or bars and virtually no shade from the sun for 30 km … for fit walkers who like space, silence and unlimited solitude … carry plenty of food and water and set out very early in the morning … not many waymarks … but easy to follow as few turnings … and like most … of the Camino, you are always walking in a straight line due west

Camino Real Francés

It is tree-lined on the sunny side and has picnic areas at intervals.

But the first is about 7 km shorter, straight to Mansilla de las Mulas: on the other hand, it doesn't go through El Burgo Ranero.

Guess which route I took?

I stopped for my usual 'fix' plus squashed banana from the depths of my rucksack at Bercianos del Real Camino. €1.50 for a medium sized café grande con leche was the highest and smallest yet: it was the only bar along the Camino where I don't think that it would matter if they didn't see any of us there again (even if we

Manfred Kress Friedrich died beside the Camino in 1998: each stone is a pilgrim's prayer

passed that way twice).

The lady behind the bar was a true product of the No Charm School Of Waiting. What a difference from the lady in the restaurant at Sahagún the previous night who, besides dealing with the bar out front and the restaurant out back, was weary but genuinely smiley throughout: and she'd had to cook my fried eggs and chips as well!

A real trouper.

Suddenly the problem became potential lack of space at El Burgo Ranero: it was listed as 26 bunks, and I was way behind the vast majority of pilgrims with whom I'd slept at Sahagún. Would they set out to do the next 20 km to Mansilla de las Mulas, and leave space for me at El Burgo Ranero? I thought that I could guess the answer: and I still stopped to take photographs as an unending line of pilgrims strode past. This had been one of the most desolate stretches of the Camino: even in the 16th century a pilgrim came across the body of another pilgrim who had been devoured by wolves. No wonder they walked in groups.

El Burgo Ranero (which meant 'the town of frogs', because it was in such a marshy area) still had it's boggy areas, and the occasional croaking on the way out.

It was now a small modern residential town with a railway station: and would you believe it, there was a train to León (39 km) next morning, at 0900, for just €1! What a lesson for Britain!

It was only just after 11.00 when I reached the Refuge: but it was already under siege.

The American/Venezuelan/Spanish couple José and Maria were up front as usual. Not surprising, as they set off each morning at 04.30: but they don't get much of the early morning views with their flashlights.

The Gloucester Girls were well placed, and lucky me, I was in 21st place. I'd made the team. Rucksacks were piled against the wall in an orderly line. It all looked very English.

The three German teachers had also made the team: everybody was happy, except those from 27 onwards in the queue.

The Refuge alleged that it didn't open until 13.00, which fooled most of the clientele, who'd decided to while away the time in the shop across the street or strolling round the village: because at 12.00 the Village Comedian, who doubled as Hospitalero, appeared with his book and table and began his one-man show (from his place in the shade) to a weary, sunbaked and increasingly exasperated audience, who really only wanted to crash into their pits for the afternoon. I rushed over to the shops to drag out José and Maria to claim their places at the front of the starting grid.

The orderly queue broke down in a dignified way rather than an unsightly stampede, people insinuating themselves up the queue rather than openly jostling frailer pilgrims out of the way: but it ended up more or less as it started, with the Village Comedian getting it just about right by reducing the waiting pilgrims into a state of weary apathy by taking so long to enter details into the register.

What's more, I even got a bottom bunk, next to the door!

I promptly took up all available floor space, washed my clothes, had a great shower, went to the shops, climbed into my bunk and promptly crashed out.

I woke in a panic. Had I overslept? Was it tomorrow?

It's a lovely little Refuge: new, bright varnished wood, sumptuous dining room where the floor sleeps goodness knows how many at a pinch, good toilet facilities, really good kitchen, a washing machine and, wait for it, four six to eight bed dormitories upstairs with ladders to the top bunks, and windows everywhere that really opened wide with shutters to keep out the glare.

I could have been happy there for ever!

Washing lines blossomed on the waste ground out the back. The spokeswoman for the three German Mothers, a charming lady who spoke excellent English, was lolling in the shade passing the time by watching the lines of washing doing not very much in the slight breeze.

'We've just had a lovely meal', she said. 'What a pity you weren't there, there was plenty for all'.

I showed signs of interest. 'But it's all gone now!' she said: 'What a pity!'

Ah well, that's part of the story of my life.

Her equally charming companion said little.

The third German Mother, who looked like a bulldog who'd swallowed a wasp, didn't speak English (in fact, I never actually heard her speak **anything**): but she showed signs of pleasure at this information.

She was the one upfront on the road, barking out the hard miles, whilst the other two sauntered behind off the pace.

The 33 km day had obviously told on this pair: they were going to catch the train to León next day, announced the spokeswoman, to help them recover further.

The Waspswallowing Bulldog looked grim at this; but unless she wanted to go it alone, she had to go along with it.

A guitarist from the Popeye School of Performing Arts was murdering a popular tune before an apathetic audience round the corner: the kitchen was full of pilgrims producing wonderful meals from raw materials: and I was waiting for the Restaurant across the road to open so that I could get my daily fix of Tubular Powders, and fried eggs and chips, topped off, of course, with a tub of yoghourt or ice cream.

Suddenly the Gloucester Girls invited me to dinner: mugs of soup, into which we spooned peas and sweetcorn from a tin, made a nourishing vegetable stew. This was followed by pancakes and a tin of peaches.

I bought the wine: I splashed out on an expensive bottle (€2.45) of rough red Rioja, in view of the occasion.

The pancakes didn't actually work. The frying pan was being used for something else, so they used a shallow saucepan to which the mixture stuck obstinately.

A lady looked in and thought it was porridge: somebody else suggested Spanish omelette. Francesc and myself spooned peach halves on to our plates and ate them whilst we waited.

The pancakes arrived, a fluffy dishful which looked like hastily scraped up scrambled egg or fried porridge: but it **tasted** like pancake, soaked in sugar and lemon juice, and it really **was** good!

It brought back memories of the meals that we were missing at home: we sat back saying 'A really good fry up, fried bread, eggs and bacon, mushrooms, beans, tomatoes … snake and pygmy pie … beans on toast', and discussing pets that we had at home (Julia had once had a pet rabbit that growled at you, she said: it would probably fetch sticks if you threw them, and bring them back to beat you), until it was time for me to wash up (yes, **again**!)

Francesc hovered attentively at my elbow: he'd never come across anything like this before, and was interested to watch.

As the evening drew in, the Village Comedian dished up a home made *gazpacho* (the traditional cold soup of Spain, made from tomatoes, onions, green peppers, cucumber and anything else that came to hand), and took over the guitar for a big sing song beside the Refuge: it was a great pilgrim evening.

Day 22
El Burgo Ranero to Mansilla de las Mulas
20 km   337 km to go

It's a new record! I was away by 05.40, and I'd have been out of town five minutes earlier if the Village Comedian (I'd asked him for directions) had told me that 'straight on' didn't mean '**straight** on', but 'straight on' if you forked left at a sort of junction after 500m instead of going 'straight on' up the minor road that was, actually, 'straight on', if you see what I mean.

But an old lady, to whom it seemed to be the most natural thing in the world to meet a lost pilgrim in the back streets at a quarter to six on a summer morning, soon put me right.

Off I went, between ditches full of croaking frogs, following the white line along the centre of the road because it was too dark to stumble along the Senda de Peregrinos at its side without a flashlight.

Muscular pilgrims striding along the footpath were giving me disapproving glances: as it was getting lighter, I shuffled unobtrusively off the road and joined them with a conciliatory smile.

They soon left me in their wake: I didn't even see them at Reliegos after 13.5 km when I stopped for my midmorning 'fix'. Funny, café con leche (grande, of course) seems to taste better the further west you go.

The Fattest Woman In Reliegos waddled in, propped herself up in the corner beside the window, and began getting her calory intake for the day under way.

I sat in the shade on the village green, watching the Village Handyman trimming the weeping willow overhead with a razor sharp sickle and a casual backhand flick.

Suddenly I heard a familiar 'Hel-**lo**, how are **you**?' as the Gloucester Girls and Francesc plonked themselves down at the nearby picnic table.

They'd left half an hour after me and caught me up without much effort.

I rummaged through my rucksack: I thought I'd got a bocadillo somewhere in there, from a couple of days ago. Ah, yes: but after careful examination, I donated it to the starving animals of Reliegos, hoping it wouldn't cause them too much distress.

What a beautiful morning! I strolled along the flat stony footpath between banks of fennel and aromatic herbs. Although the road was so close, the landscape around must have been the same for centuries. It was as if time had stood still. I savoured the experience, the sun washing the golden landscape: sadly, it will soon be overtaken by 'progress'.

Mansilla de las Mulas, shimmering in the distance across the flat plain, was only 6.5 km away: it might have been on the other side of the world, for all I cared at that moment.

I stopped to pick some interesting-looking seeds, from a plant that resembled a spiky grass with big hairy seed heads like a rabbit's tail. I'll sow them and see what comes up.

I gathered a few, full of spiky seeds with sharp pointy ends, and put them into my top shirt pocket, where the rucksack strap crossed. Big mistake: every time I twitched to the left, I got multiple sharp stabs in my left ... well, er ... chest, you know, in the sticky out bit in the middle.

It wasn't long before I transferred the seeds to the back pocket of my bum bag, which lies across my stomach: and I still couldn't get rid of the last couple, that had embedded themselves deep into the fabric of my shirt, until I reached the Refuge an hour and a half later.

Goodness knows what trials and tribulations the early plant collectors must have experienced in the wilds of Tibet, a hundred years or more ago: possibly even worse than me now.

A kilometre outside Mansilla, I was overtaken by my first Walkman on the Camino: and minutes later by a familiar 'Hello' as the Gloucester Girls and Francesc swept by, and led the 'peloton' through the streets to the Refuge, packing tightly as a team and almost certainly in the top twelve.

We'd arrived by 10.30. I felt knotted up with guilt for not pressing on the further 20 km to León. The longer I stood and thought, the less time remained, and the more chance there was of the Refuge in León being **full!**

Soon, I didn't feel at all guilty: in fact, by midday it seemed I'd taken the only sensible decision.

José and Maria, as ever, were at the front of the patient queue outside the front door: not surprising, as they started each day at 04.30 with their tiny backpacks (how I envied them!)

They were a beautiful couple, thirty seven years married: Venezuelans who'd lived in America for years (mind you, you'd never have guessed from José's command of English, which was about the same as my command of Spanish, so I had to communicate via Maria whenever we sat together for a chat), they'd come to Spain, settled near Murcia in the south and now enjoyed themselves walking. They were enviably happy together: they just lived for each other, immersed in each other's company: and they spent most of their time at the Refuges cooking small vegetarian meals, massaging each other's feet, and strolling round the town holding hands in the intervals between.

I was going to lose them at León, because they wanted to spend a day there. I was going to lose the Gloucester Girls there as well. They were flying home: and the faithful Francesc, their own personal Sancho Panza, was going to spend a day there with his grandmother and take the Gloucester Girls round for tea.

I hoped she wasn't going to draw the wrong conclusions.

The Refuge was tucked away in an old narrow street off the main square, upper stories of the houses leaning outwards in an attempt to reach each other.

I left my rucksack in the street, stacked amongst the others, twelfth in the queue: the odd resting pilgrim would keep an eye on them all as he sat and dozed. You felt **that** safe on the Camino: although you heard occasional stories of how this trust had been destroyed (it would be foolish anyway, for instance, not to have kept your valuables with you all the time, and tucked down your sleeping bag at night), it was still an almost unthinkable occurrence.

I wandered through the square and into an upmarket Café/bar looking for a cheese bocadillo: old habits die hard. 'It's off!' said the No Charm School Waitress. She offered a pizza. Bit early for that: I settled for my usual (café con leche grande, with lots of sugar of course) before I went scouting round looking for places to get Pilgrim Meals and also, to find the way out of town next morning.

The Hospitalero was one of the nicest men that I was to meet: a tall, spare, grey haired man, who had walked the Camino himself many times and who couldn't do enough to help pilgrims in need of advice or repair.

Dormitories surrounded the central courtyard, upstairs, downstairs, little toilets and washrooms tucked into odd corners. You could sit upstairs in the Hospitalero's toilet and get a clear unobstructed view of the entire courtyard below: it was one of the most peaceful that I had ever occupied, but you couldn't really use it at night because a couple of cyclists were sleeping in there. The landings and stairwells were full, too. Space is at a premium in early August.

The cold showers, interspersed with an occasional invigorating flash of hot water, were out of this world.

I washed my clothes, and hung them on the cluttered lines beside the deep sinks with their sloping scrubbing boards: you had to do a little adjustment of odd bits of other people's washing to get enough space.

I sat in the old courtyard, shaded by a huge fig tree. Pilgrims sat around talking and inspecting each other's feet: the smell of spicy meals being prepared in the kitchen wafted over from the open window. A sunbattered pilgrim sat at my side, eyes closed in silent contemplation, soaking his feet in the washing up bowl from the kitchen.

I dripped hot Kitkat on my shorts, washed them out at the sink, and sat in my underpants watching them steam dry on the table in front of me.

Cyclists began to queue outside in the narrow road: like many Refuges, they weren't admitted until 17.30, which meant that they were usually the guys who clogged up the kitchen floor and the corridors on their sleeping mats, and got their own back by refusing to rise until about 07.30.

The Gloucester Girls (and Francesc!) invited me to join them for a meal around the long wooden table in the kitchen.

We'd also been joined by Jack The Lad.

'Bet you can't guess where I come from, from me accent?', he hazarded: 'Go on, give it a guess!'

'Begins with L', he added helpfully.

It seemed vaguely familiar. Leicester, perhaps?

Turned out to be London. He'd been pushing on, 40 km a day, trying to get a decent drink of cider.

Cider was his passion.

He'd been to Murphy's in Sahagún.

'Nice enough bloke, told me cider wasn't beer. Well, I knew **that!'**

I thought of telling him that Eduardo Murphy was my uncle, and that we called him Uncle Eddie, but decided against it.

He was just trying to hustle on to Galicia, where he heard that they produced great cider. He gave away his biscuits, and departed in a whirlwind of crumbs.

I never saw him again.

The Gloucester Girls had cooked a big saucepan of asparagus soup, so we all had a basin of this: then spaghetti with peas and sweetcorn, spiced up with asparagus soup: a few of Jack the Lad's biscuits: then out for an ice cream in the treelined main square.

It was Saturday evening, families in their best clothes sitting on the many benches beside the surrounding walls and around the cool fountain, whilst the children played on their bicycles welcomed or chastised by all and sundry, one huge extended family in the security of their own town square. It was Spain as it had been for centuries.

We felt like intruders.

I was in the French end of the dormitory.

Unfortunately, it included The World's Greatest Snorer, Simian (Simeon?). Anyway, that's what I called him, because he had all the characteristics of the more hairy of the great apes apart from the fact that he wore glasses. Oh, and I don't know whether or not he had a tail: I didn't like to inspect him too closely in the showers.

Why 'Simian', when his real name turned out to be Rafael? Ah well, it's a good crossword clue: but I had to check it out in the dictionary to be sure!

He varied the timbre and tone of his performance with considerable subtlety: sometimes great basso profundo offerings that lasted for minutes on end, sometimes little playful whimpers, whilst occasionally he would lie silent, gathering his strength for one enormous blast ending in a strangled snort. It was impressive.

At the other end of the dormitory, a rotund little lady kept up a background accompaniment with little whinnying whistles and the occasional gasp and grunt.

I awoke at 01.15, and didn't really get to sleep again.

Most of the dormitory was awake by then anyway, flashing torches directly into his eyes from distant bunks to try to stop the performance: but it was in vain. But we were all so well behaved that we didn't like to interfere directly with his right to life.

So the long night continued until a pilgrim dropped a trekking pole from a top bunk and everybody got up. I'll say one thing: the shock stopped Simian snoring.

Day 23
Mansilla de las Mulas to León
19 km   317 km to go

It was Sunday. The French sat around noisily in the courtyard: the English sat around the wooden table in the kitchen. The cyclists stayed in their sleeping bags.

Francesc had his three cupfuls of Nampa Zampa (chocolate crispies) and milk.

I was away late: the bar at Puente Villarente, only 6 km down the road, was already packed with pilgrims and locals by the time I arrived at 08.15.

The Guide Books don't give the route **after** this long straggly town a very good press. 'Hard to follow', it said.

Well, maybe in the past: but not now.

A kilometre beyond the town, you cross the road and a wide well-marked path leads for 6 km to a tidy sparkling village, Valdelafuente, and rejoins the busy main road 6 km later.

Regular blasts of gun fire from a stadium far below echoed in the morning air.

As I climbed the final rocky hill to Valdafuente at 1015 in searing heat, a squat muscular lady, obviously built to last, was raking up scrub-like hay in to a stack with the size of rake that we usually pull behind tractors in England. I didn't envy her the remaining five acres or so: but I suppose that she'd got into her stride, and who would want to stop her now?

It's a pity that Jack The Lad wasn't sitting on the shady concrete bench at my side, beneath the shady trees beside the fountain in the tiny square, because there was a BIG notice in large letters pointing to the bar with the words *Hoy sidra natural* ('We sell home brewed cider').

He hadn't needed to go all the way to Galicia after all: and the cider turned out to be delicious.

I thought I'd better make a move, when a repulsive small dog kept making suggestive inroads on my day-old jam and primula bocadillo. It's face looked as though it had run into a wall at speed, with subsequent reconstructive surgery proving ineffectual. A group of pilgrims were holding a private service in the shade beside the fountain.

Their responses were very moving.

After the next quiet 6 km along rough tracks, I faced a very different kilometre along the hard shoulder of the busy N630, with León basking in the sun below.

Suddenly I forgot where I was: the sight of a man in a fast approaching car, sitting in what (in England) would be the 'driving seat', and rubbing his eyes with both hands at once, almost made me leap for cover over the crash barrier until I realised that we were in continental Europe, where they drive on the right, and that this guy was a **passenger**! Phew!

I was heading for the Refuge in the Benedictine Convent ('Lady monks', as Francesc remarked), which was not only on the far side of the centre of the city, but very close to his grandmother's house.

I looked carefully at the team of massed Hospitaleros around the long table, laden with welcoming jugs of water and orange juice, beneath the archway leading to the big, enclosed courtyard.

There seemed a familiar face in the team. I found later that 'Sister Agatha', now in civvies, had been seconded there from Santo Domingo de la Calzada, twelve days back down the Camino, presumably to 'spice up' the team.

She sternly informed us all that **NOBODY** could leave the

Convent before 06.00 next morning, and if they imagined otherwise, they had another think coming!

I imagined that at 06.00, there would be a mass start, trekking poles flailing, last one out's a cissy: and all the time, the pilgrims down the road in the Municipal Refuge down by the river would be stealing a march on us, grabbing those few precious bunks at Villadangos del Paramo.

What's more, she continued, the doors closed at 9.30 pm sharp at night: no excuses accepted!

The only exemption was for those who had followed the parade from the Convent to the church for the late Mass: and they, I assumed, would be returning under escort.

She took me up to the dormitory, probably to see if I constituted some security risk or whether I was likely to be well enough behaved.

I asked if there was a bread shop or a supermarket nearby.

She reeled back with shock: I thought that she was going to have to grab the nearest bunk for support.

'It is **Sunday**, you know!' she replied icily. Of course, I nodded.

The dormitories, fitted out with sturdy metal bunks, well spaced out, were up on the first floor.

For the first time, men and women pilgrims were segregated, big dormitories separated by the washrooms (although so far I hadn't seen any surreptitious hanky-panky to set the pulse racing). After all, we were **Pilgrims**.

Wonderful hot showers: a nice 'kitchen' in which to eat, but no cooking facilities.

This didn't bother me one bit, because apart from warming up a packet of soup **once**, I'd been able to resist (quite easily) the temptation to cook in these first twenty three days. But now it might be a bit different, because I would no longer be able to hoover up the Gloucester Girls' leftovers or grab Shamak's leftover stew.

León is effectively closed on Sundays.

It's the ideal place for the Lord's Day Observance Society to go for a weekend break.

But it's definitely not the place to be if you're short of food, and without friends to visit: and I certainly fitted into these categories. It was alright if you were big on self sufficiency: but pretty dismal if you were out of stock, of course.

I'd managed to buy a small loaf at the bar, mid-morning, and I wandered round the streets nibbling it and feeling generally hungry, as I looked for a stray corner-shop.

A man smiled and gestured to me to follow him. I wandered along behind him (not close enough for people to think that we were in any way connected), and he led me straight to – a bread shop. Just bread: and cakes.

It didn't seem diplomatic to go in with my half eaten loaf: so I thanked him, and left.

I ate the remains of my bread, daubed with jam and primula, and a stray biscuit left over from Jack The Lad's donation.

I slumped on my pillowless bunk and dozed for a couple of hours. Washing done, and a prime place bagged for drying, a warm shower, a midday meal and a doze: what more, I asked myself not for the first time, could any man want?

I walked up to the magnificent cathedral later, passing the famed Gaudi building on the way.

Visitors, apparently, come from miles around to view it.

Well, I like (some) modern art and architecture, but **this** building – I searched my vocabulary for the right word and could only come up with 'grotesque' and, I suppose, 'gaudy', which seemed very apposite.

It looked like one of the brightly painted toy castles with which we used to play as children, set incongruously in a mediaeval setting.

I can't imagine what could have possessed a mega-rich family to have had it designed and built: and, having viewed the finished product, been thick skinned enough to live there. Me, I'd have said (after recovering from the initial shock), on seeing it for the first time, 'Now come on, stop mucking about, show me what you've **really** done! Is it behind this screen?'

The cathedral, high on the hill, dominates the city.

Inside, it is almost surreal. The stained glass windows, the length and height of this huge building, are almost beyond comprehension. I stood for a long time, asking myself 'How did they do this?'

Primitive craftsmen, with the most highly developed skills, fuelled by their beliefs: one window could take a lifetime to create, and the colouring was so vibrant and alive.

I sat and meditated for a long time. Tears, as ever, came easily.

The cathedral at León

I watched The Worst Driver In Spain preparing for the European Championships later in the year. Five attempts to reverse into a double sized parking space beside the road, with his friend behind, guiding him in. Sometimes he attacked slowly, sometimes at speed: sometimes he started from the centre of the road, sometimes he avoided the car in front by a mere hairsbreadth as he took a more shallow approach. His wife sat placidly at his side: even the slow squeal of rubber on kerb didn't perturb her.

He paused, preparing for a sixth attempt.

I wandered away: I felt that I was intruding on a private family grief.

The Gloucester Girls decided to have a night out, as it was to be their last night on the Camino this year. We took pictures in the dormitory, arms round each other as we leant on the iron bunks.

Julia chose a Burger King for the celebration, which was apparently defying the embargo on Sunday food sales for which Sister Agatha had hoped.

We walked there through the little streets: every alley, every square, was lined with tables and chairs outside dark little restaurants, thronged with people relaxing, laughing and talking on this hot summer evening. Street musicians wandered from bar to bar. It was still the Spain that I remembered from forty years ago.

But back to business. I had a Big One – and some onion rings, deep fried in batter: it tasted very Burger Kingy.

We hurried back to the Refuge, guided by Francesc whose navigational skills proved very substandard. 9.20: ten minutes to curfew, and I still hadn't bought a bottle of orange for tomorrow. The others were fairly ambivalent about this: after all, they were

The Gloucester Girls and Francesc

going to see Francesc's grandmother tomorrow.

9.25: we tumbled in through the door of the Refuge to safety.

I was packed and lying on my bunk, nodding off in my ragged singlet, when the Gloucester Girls (and Francesc) appeared at the foot of my bunk to say goodbye.

I know I should have done the decent thing and got up, but they sort of took me by surprise. All I could do was pull down my ragged singlet to cover my robust Marks and Spencer y-fronts (£6.99 for a pack of three), and shuffle under my sleeping bag. I waved, and wished them all the best: I heard them giggling as they went into the ladies dormitory.

I would have done the same.

Suddenly, my heart did a somersault.

The occupant of the next bunk, with which mine was locked together to save space, crashed onto his mattress and put the springs under considerable stress.

It was Simian, the World's Greatest Snorer: and throughout the night, not only would his head be only 18 inches from mine, but his Snoring Equipment would be pointing in my direction!

I had to get into a deep sleep first. No such luck: Simian was asleep in five seconds flat: a low whistle, followed by a rumble, seemed a portent of things to come.

But they **didn't** come!

Perhaps he'd played himself out yesterday, even kept himself awake so that he now needed his sleep: whatever, he was obviously saving himself to defend his World Title and was satisfied with his workout the previous night.

I lay awake for hours, waiting for him to start: it was almost worse than his virtuoso recital at Mansilla. I finally drifted off: the rest of the dormitory, mindful of Sister Agatha's dire warning, slept until 05.00. Not a man stirred.

The Bleak Páramo

Day 24
León to San Martín del Camino
24 km   298 km to go

Noise and activity slowly increased: by 5.45 we were gathering for a massed start beneath the archway. It was like the start of the London Marathon: elite walkers at the front, toes caressing the starting line impatiently, and the rest of the mob lurking at the back hoping for the best.

But, would you believe it, José and Maria and a few others had already 'gone over the wall' so to speak, and escaped early. Sister Agatha, in sensible tweeds, looked grim.

If it had been a doddle getting **to** the Refuge, with signs on every street corner, it was a different matter getting **out** of León. It was the complete opposite to Burgos.

By 06.15, hundreds (well, not hundreds exactly, probably dozens: oh well, seven or eight) of pilgrims were milling about the nearby square, looking for a clue.

A street sweeper came along to help, until a Man Who Had Walked The Camino Before took charge and guided us through the gardens outside the Hotel San Marcos, over the bridge and through the industrial and residential areas.

He was moving pretty fast, so it soon stretched the pack out behind. It was quite invigorating for an early morning.

The rules for Getting Out Of A City are:

1) Find someone who knows the way and stick close behind him until you can find the signs yourself

2) Ditch him

We were at the end of the seemingly endless *meseta* at León: now came the equally flat but even more desolate *páramo*.

But before this came a 6 km uphill grind through the apparently unregulated linear sprawl that has transformed the León that I knew, until we reached the mandatory bar at Virgen del Camino. Coffee, of course: and a cheese bocadillo. After a couple of bites, I thoughtfully put it away for later.

Just out of the town, you had the option of taking either the Road Option, through Villadangos del Páramo, or the Country Route, through Villar de Mazarife.

I sat and considered it all carefully.

I was glad to see that my Guide Book described the Road Route as 'traditional': my heart warmed to the writer when I read this.

The Country Route was 'somewhat sparsely waymarked, but easy enough to follow'. I wished they'd missed out the qualifying clause: it introduced the need for a decision, something I try to avoid.

Oh yes: as my finger tracked down the page and added up distances, I found that it was 12 km further along the Country Route to Hospital de Orbigo, my original goal for the day.

So it was no contest, in the end: I'd walk beside the road, through the villages with their names that rolled mellifluously off the tongue: Valverde de la Virgen (almost 3,000 ft above sea level, and bone chillingly cold in winter), San Miguel del Camino, Villadangos del Páramo, San Martín del Camino: these little settlements through the barren desolate *páramo* bound the Camino together.

I thought of stopping at Villadangos now: but persistent adverts for the 'new' Refuge at San Martín del Camino, which would put me a nice attainable 24 km from Astorga the next day, settled it for me.

Soon I was sitting beside the fountain at San Miguel del Camino, under the shade of the trees beside a high freestanding belltower which, besides supporting two enormous bells which looked as if they would destroy the whole building if both swung the same way at the same time, was topped with four huge stork nests.

Both my cameras ran out of film at this point: I sat restocking them and thinking how lucky I was, sitting beneath the Spanish sun in a setting

Storks at home in San Miguel del Camino

that had probably not changed for four hundred years.

How sad I was, also, that Myfanwy was not with me: but she's always there, holding my hand. So I must keep doing my best for her, and for the boys and their families. Walking the Camino might seem a funny way to do this: but to me, it's very real.

I was galvanised into action when the Gang Of Twelve sauntered past.

If places were going to be tight, this might be the decider: and I didn't fancy a mattress on the floor after 24 km.

José and Maria were waiting for me at Villadangos, to show me the way to the small cosy Refuge. They had decided not to stay in León, but had pressed on to Villadangos.

I was set on pressing on to San Martín. We said our farewells: I liked them very much, and will miss them. We shook hands: as I looked back down the road, they were still standing there, and waved.

I was still tracking the Gang Of Twelve relentlessly: and just before San Martín, they sat down around a ruined house for a snack and a snooze. The ladies were just going round the back to look at the garden: and with a brisk 'Hola!' I was gone.

I even stopped at a petrol station for a Nestea, looking over my shoulder anxiously.

I turned in through the gate of the new Refuge. Bit of an anticlimax, as I was only about the tenth arrival at an 80 bed Refuge, and even more disappointing when the Gang Of Twelve strode past.

Even the French Connection, sitting having a brew in the Refuge garden, decided to press on, and got up and left.

The new Refuge remained obstinately empty: yet it was not a bad deal at €3. It just hadn't made it's way into the Guide Books yet, which probably took years.

A German group arrived, who had left Villadangos because it wasn't 'interesting'.

I said that this wasn't 'interesting' either: more important, it was clean with **hot** showers.

True, there wasn't much in the way of pots and pans: you find more at an English Jumble Sale, but as I said before 'What do you want for €3?'

And you get lots of flies; not enough people to share them out, but as long as you kept moving, you were alright.

'Why do you sleep beside the door?' a German began his cross-examination.

'Because I can get out easily, and don't disturb anybody else if I leave early'.

Um, yes: he could see the validity of this.

'But you are next to the passage: everybody will walk past and keep you awake'.

'I don't mind: I sleep easily'.

He gave up: haven't seen him since. Perhaps I wasn't interesting, either.

He was probably on one of the bunks up on the stage (it obviously doubled as the village hall in winter); I hope the scaffolding holding up the bunks doesn't come crashing down into the auditorium during the night. Now, **that** really **would** wake me up!

Ada and her Hulk, Reiner, who I had met briefly the previous day in León, sitting hunched up on the Tourist Sightseeing Train waiting for a group of excited children to climb aboard, were already in residence. They'd bagged a couple of bunks just inside the entrance.

I was hungry, and the remnants of a cheese bocadillo didn't seem to fit the bill, although I made a valiant attempt. Time for the packet of chicken soup that I'd been saving for just such an emergency.

I hate these electric stoves: how can you simmer for fifteen minutes on a ring that is glowing red, and takes an hour to be cool enough to touch? It was made more difficult by the fact that the only pan had no handle: just a slot where one could be fitted.

Delia would have admired the way I kept lifting the pan off, cupping it in my spare shorts, whenever it began to boil over and after a decent interval, putting it back on.

The fifteen minutes took almost half an hour.

Now I only had three hours to wait until the Supermarket rumbled into activity and the bar opened for meals. Supermarket, by the way, is a contradiction in terms: it is never 'super' and is what we would call 'a corner shop', the essential hub of these small villages.

Reiner uncoiled himself off the top bunk: I thought he was never going to stop, about two metres (six foot six) tall, and a face with a permanently startled expression topped with a ragged fringe of hair around a bald centre. His face probably couldn't work out why it was so far off the ground, and found the sensation somewhat disconcerting.

Reiner and Ada suggested that we should go out for a meal together.

It didn't seem to be something that the bar did every day.

After a hasty discussion with the regulars, a table was cleared in an alcove beyond the bar, and mats and cutlery put in place. But it was alright: a pot of macaroni was already bubbling on the stove, and soon achieved the familiar rubbery texture of a pilgrim starter.

San Martín was the Fly Capital Of The World.

The restaurant floor was a seething kaleidoscope of them, until darkness fell and they all mysteriously disappeared. Where they went, I don't know: probably getting in an early night ready for a prompt start pestering pilgrims next day.

Ada confided that she couldn't stand flies, but that she didn't mind cockroaches ('They don't do anything to you') and, after all, she'd shared a flat with thousands of them in Sydney.

Well, they do things to me, like making my flesh creep, especially when one dropped out of the light fitting onto my desk at Kew Gardens and crawled off towards the door. It didn't make it.

And they're excellent carriers of diseases, as well.

But it's OK, folks, I never met one along the Camino.

Reiner inspected me at length.

Finally he spoke. 'Did your arms achieve this colour on the Camino?'

Yes, I agreed, they did.

This cheered him up. He quizzed me about English weather ('Is it true that it rains for eight months of the year?'): well, I wasn't going to let the side down, so I explained the subtle differences between Continental Europe and Island (British) climates. It sounded pretty convincing to **me**, anyway, and could well be right.

He also wanted to know why rugby isn't popular in Germany: but since he was surprised to hear that they played the game in New Zealand, it would be a hard job to explain the worldwide appeal of the game, as typified by such subtle exponents of the art as Martin Johnson and Jason Leonard, and discuss the difficulties in attracting advertising sponsorship to market the game to an audience with similar background knowledge to himself, so I just made general noises and left it at that.

Back at the Refuge, lights went **on** at 10.30 when a group of talkative French pilgrims decided to pack and chat. One solicitously enquired whether I was having a good night: I explained that the only thing preventing this was the light being on, and gradually it all subsided.

This was one of those (few) times when I longed for the assertive presence of Sister Agatha.

Day 25
San Martín del Camino to Astorga
24 km   274 km to go

I was up at 05.00, packed, and into the kitchen for breakfast half an hour later. A French lady was sleeping on the floor behind the door: I know, I should have turned on the light and provoked an international incident, but I didn't have the nerve. I got by in the dull light of the coffee and chocolate machine, which delivered sweet brown slurry in strange, different flavours for a mere €0.50.

The Hospitalero appeared just before 06.00 to prepare breakfast for her paying guests: (€3 in advance, so it didn't really matter if you turned up or not). The French lady sighed and went off somewhere else. I don't know why she was sleeping there anyway, when she had sixty empty bunks next door from which to choose.

One pilgrim appeared at 06.00, to plaster his feet: everybody else still slept.

When I left ten minutes later, not a sound disturbed the enormous dormitory.

Reiner and Ada had intended to leave at 05.00: but as Ada was having major foot problems since resting up in a cosy hotel at León, waiting to meet and greet Reiner after he'd flown in from Germany, I wasn't surprised that both were still snoring when I left.

I was tempted to turn on the lights and shout 'Wakey, wakey!', but as I'm British I just crept out and away.

The Hospitalero surveyed her enormous pan of boiling milk and, like the French lady, also sighed.

The first 7 km, most of it on a footpath beside the road with the odd detour through shady country lanes, took me into Hospital de Orbigo. You'll be absolutely fascinated to know, I'm sure, that to reach the town I had to cross the Longest Pilgrim Bridge In Spain: 204 metres long, twenty arches!

Now, you'll **also** be fascinated to hear (won't you?) about the Not Much Risk Jousting Tournament which took place there in 1434.

I'd thought that jousting was a pretty dangerous sport: but after a month of competition, in which 300 lances were broken, mercifully only one contestant died.

Doesn't say much for the quality of lances used, though.

But I didn't stop, even for my usual 'fix': I carried on manfully.

I'd hoped to catch up with José and Maria, but no such luck.

At Hospital de Orbigo, I cracked and decided to take the Country Route (even though it was 1 km further) to San Justo de la Vega. I'd had enough, for the time being, of road walking and lorry dodging.

After a week of Beside The Road Walking, it was hard going. The sun was high, the hills were steep and the track was stony, at first through market gardens and then through evergreen oak woods for the 12 km to San Justo.

It was magical to sink into a seat outside a café and hear the laughter of the pilgrims inside. Bit late for a coffee stop, really: and the café con leche grande was getting **less** grande, and the cost **more** grande, the further west I walked. So I boosted it with a chocolate cake and a can of Nestea. Bernard from Dublin sank into a neighbouring chair

Only 3 km to Astorga, all off road until I began to climb the hill between the steeply stacked houses.

It was market day: I had to force my sweaty way through the crowded streets, with stalls down each side. It was the longest and narrowest street market that I had ever seen. I wish I'd been able to snap up the bargains: three towels for €6 seemed pretty good to me, but I guess I'd never have carried them home.

A police lady, handcuffs tucked into her belt and irritated by my lack of understanding, gave me a personal escort through the battling throng of shoppers to the broad esplanade, above the tiny packed houses beneath and with fantastic views over the distant mountains, which led direct to the 232 bed Refuge.

At 1 pm, I was still one of the first arrivals.

The Refuge at Astorga is massive but featureless, but very comfortable. Lots of showers, bags of room to do the washing, and a courtyard full of lines and open plan driers. There's also a smaller Refuge nearby, tucked into the narrow streets close to the cathedral and the shops, which looked really cosy. Most of my 'friends' were there, I found later, when I met them wandering round the square.

I visited the cathedral, next to another hideous Gaudi building: and this 'eyesore' is compounded (to me, but then I'm rather bigoted) with a Gaudi museum across the square. A mausoleum might have been a better idea!

I did my shopping for breakfast: one banana (yellow!), one orange (both weighed out and carefully priced), one yoghourt, one *media pan* (small loaf of bread), three or four B & B sized packets of jam, the Spanish version of Primula, a can of *cas limón* (gassy lemon drink), a small bar of white chocolate for which I had developed an insatiable lust and which I sat outside and ate in it's entirety. A pack of salami. A square of cake, as well: oh yes, my 'insurance policy' of a packet of chicken soup. I would have bought a different flavour, but I didn't understand the names on the packets: I'm not into dangerous living.

Had I enough money? €4 (£2.50)? Believe me, I know what self catering is like when there's no expense spared.

But this 'self catering' doesn't extend to cooking: that's heavy stuff, and just not economical anyway when you're by yourself on the Camino.

So it was a pilgrim meal. How nice to get a good plateful of **real** tinned spaghetti in tomato sauce (just like Sainsbury's), followed by a slab of rubbery tired tortilla (playdough) and salad. The huge segment of melon that followed would have been great had it been fully ripe, but it was still pretty good, and I felt full: and at €6.75, you can't complain (and I mean this sincerely, folks!). Unlimited wine: and bread, of course.

Another storm was brewing up over the mountains to the west beyond distant Rabanal. I went for a long walk along the esplanade, packed with families with children in pushchairs, very often with parents and grandparents within this family group: or old people just sitting resting, thinking, gazing, on the benches alongside the walls, or walking slowly along.

I looked down over the small houses, fascinated by their individual and intimate gardens reflecting the lives of the people who lived there, imagining their lives from what I could see before me. Then through the public gardens, borders packed with mature attractive shrubs, past the shaded bandstand and the café at it's side full of people relaxing in the early evening. The narrow streets beyond were now empty: the street market might never have existed. The golden dusk, distant storm clouds rolling across the sky, was closing down the day.

'People watching': an absorbing pastime.

Lights out at 10.30. Nobody snored: but I woke just after

midnight and endured one of those nights when sleep wouldn't come.

I lay and did sums in my head: less than 33% of the Camino remained to walk, 510 km walked in 25 days, 20.4 km per day … I fell into an uneasy sleep, thunder rumbling in the distance and the sky lit by distant lighting, until an alarm went off. Then it was all go!

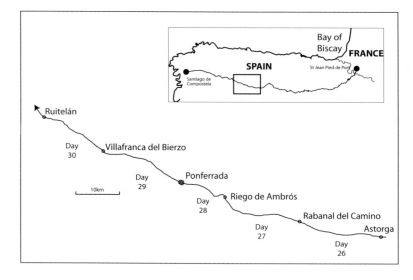

9

The Even Bleaker Maragatería

Day 26

Astorga to Rabanal del Camino

19 km   250 km to go

I was heading into the mountains, through the bleak, beautiful
maragatería (bleaker than the *páramo* which preceded it, and
which in its turn was bleaker than the *meseta* before **that**) all the
way to the Cruz de Ferro, the highest point of the Camino at
more than 1,500 metres (almost 5,000 ft).

Nobody knows the origins of the *maragatos*, the people who
lived in this region: perhaps Phoenicians, perhaps Berbers from
the 9th century.

But they were a race apart: for centuries they were the
muleteers, the 'hard men' of the Spanish transport system, until
they were superceded by 38 tonne trucks.

Those 50 km across the mountains to Ponferrada are a long
hard trek: and if you're doing it in one session, it's basically
uphill for 30 km and basically downhill for the next 20. Even in
summer you may need warm clothes and waterproofs.
Unfortunately, I'd sent most of mine back from Pamplona: I'd

just got a perforated vest and a boil-in-the-bag raintop tucked into my rucksack.

Good job it was the hottest, driest summer for years.

But, remember to take plenty of water and food: it's hard to come by for the next few miles.

It was a steady 9 km climb along a dirt track to Santa Catalina de Somoza; no, they didn't sell them at the bar, I asked, so I settled for my usual fix.

A French pilgrim strode past, eyes fixed firmly ahead, four toilet rolls in a supermarket bag suspended from his staff.

Either he was on a rescue mission, or he knew something that I didn't.

'Relief and 'Mafeking' came to mind.

I hadn't meant to stop again: but – the bar at El Ganso was something else!

Not only did he sell *sidra natural* (hope Jack The Lad had called!), but El Mesón Cowboy (the Cowboy Bar) was a monument to the Mid West of America and not so subtle marketing, slap bang in the centre of rural Spain.

On the wall, between saddles, stirrups and cowboy hats, was a large framed feature recounting the story of the man who had walked the entire 774 km of the Camino (760 km if you follow my guide book, but I'm willing to come round to his way of thinking) from St Jean last year in 12 days!

I knew there'd be a record, somewhere, although I doubt that they'd plaster it up on the walls at Santiago as it didn't appear to leave much time for quiet reflection. Might get into the Guinness Book of Records, though.

No, I won't mention his name (actually, I've forgotten it anyway), because anything further from the spirit of the Camino is hard to imagine. But it's a pretty good effort …

I lingered for half an hour, sipped a can of *cas limón* sitting

Mesón Cowboy: a monument to the mid-west

on the old wooden bench beneath the shade of the vines overhead in the garden, and chatting with the Young Spanish Lady Now Living In Essex And Working In An Advertising Agency In London and her friends. Her American accent was a little hard to follow at times: but she was a great girl!

After that, it was a steady grind to Rabanal del Camino, finishing with the ascent of the vertical village street.

But what an interesting grind! The whole nature of the vegetation began to change.

Aromatic Cistus, yellow broom, heather and ling (*Calluna vulgaris*) were flowering beside the road. Tree heathers, up to 2 m (7 ft) high, dotted the fringes of the open pine woods mingling with the denser oak woodland which had developed from the scattered clumps dotting the bare, open *páramo*: steep valleys, a sea of yellow and mauve in the spring, stretched to the hazy distant mountains.

Once upon a time, Rabanal had been a thriving village with

three churches and a *hospital* (as opposed to a hospital, with or without A & E), an important pilgrim halt: now it has a population of twenty eight, except (of course) in summer when it comes to life again. I guess, at 1149 m (3,750 ft) it's pretty bleak in winter: not a good bet for a retirement home!

The Refugio Gaucelmo, just across from the church, is **our** refuge: it was converted to a Refuge from the Priest's house by the Confraternity of St James (to which I am proud to belong) and is now staffed by volunteers from the Confraternity through the season. But, it doesn't open until 2.30pm: almost three hours away.

Half a dozen sweaty pilgrims sat outside in the shade, led by Bernard, who had made a special effort to leave Astorga early to guarantee himself a bunk. As it turned out, he needn't have bothered. They were facing a three hour wait, unless they whiled away the time in nearby bars with such beckoning titles as The Genuine Refuge.

I was hot, I was weary: I wandered down to the village square, alongside the main road from which I'd climbed earlier, and found two newish super Refuges (at least I suppose the second was super as well, the Albergue Rabanal del Camino, a name which was functional rather than inspirational).

Mine certainly was: the Albergue del Pilar.

Write it in letters two feet high (they do, actually, on the wall at the front).

It's built around a shady rural courtyard: the cool dormitories with their wooden bunks, toilets and showers which both do as they promise, a line of sinks, rows of drying racks and, once you've sorted yourself out, a long shady bar that serves good, reasonably priced meals so that pilgrims can eat and enjoy a drink at leisure.

And all for €4! Just the place to catch up on a good night's

Luxury at the Albergue del Pilar, Rabanal

sleep!

Magnus from Madrid, only 18, introduced me to *empanada*: he broke off a corner of his for me to taste.

Good *empanada*, a flat pie filled with meat or fish and vegetables, served warm and juicy, is great: even cold, squashed flat *empanada* (usually filled with tuna, which I love) and chopped up into slabs in bars along the Camino, is pretty good.

This was **great**: in fact, it was **five star great.** I was straight up to the bar in case they ran out of stock.

Magnus had been to school in Switzerland, and had taken his A levels in English.

He'd even been persuaded to play rugby – once. It figured high on his list of Things Not To Do Twice.

He'd heard of Jonah Lomu: how big was he? REALLY? Wow! And he also knew that the All Blacks came from New Zealand, so his education was now almost complete.

He was walking the Camino to 'find himself', and also for the challenge, not from any religious viewpoint.

Had he found himself? Yes: but what he'd found, he didn't say.

I retired to my bunk for the afternoon: the dormitory throbbed to regular pilgrim breathing.

Magnus had long since set off for Foncebadón, high up on the slopes of the highest point of the Camino.

Suddenly a Crash! disturbed my reverie.

Thunder and lightning had come early today. They had been my distant evening companions for days: now they were directly overhead, and rain was thrashing down onto the Refuge. Such storms, apparently, were frequent along the Camino in August.

My washing! All the clothes that I possessed on the Camino were either on **me**, or on the drying racks!

But the Hospitalero, bless his little cotton and artificial fibre mix socks, had whisked the driers under cover. He was certainly earning his €4 the hard way.

After the rain stopped, pilgrims sat outside inspecting their own and their friends feet gloomily. It looked like chimpanzees in a David Attenborough wildlife documentary doing intrapersonal grooming.

Many of them had started from León so that they could cunningly avoid the *meseta*, only to find that they'd still got to cross the *páramo* and then the *maragatería*, both of which must have been quite a nasty shock for unprepared feet.

But you can pick out the new pilgrims: they generally have a feet fixation, and go up and down steps one foot at a time, drawing the other up to meet it before taking on the next step, often moaning silently (you know what I mean, you're just being difficult).

It's a stage that can last for up to ten days.

The old hands (or, I suppose, feet) swagger about, striding up steps (sometimes without even grasping the handrail), going for long invigorating walks around the village and popping in to bars to pinch toilet paper or paper napkins for the next day.

Their pockets are always bulging.

You can often find them sitting casually rubbing Vaseline into their feet with a brisk no-nonsense attitude, and showing off large healing blisters to new pilgrims with a nonchalant air.

A gnarled pilgrim, according to his T shirt a veteran of the Valencia Marathon, was showing unfit pilgrims, who'd had a couple of hours to cool down and stiffen up, how to pull muscles by showing them how to do stretches.

A potbellied pilgrim and his wife and daughter appeared to have survived unscathed.

The gnarled pilgrim, happy that he'd Done His Bit To Teach Fitness Training To The Unfit, returned to his beer, cigarettes and cards with a modest smile, brushing aside thanks.

Ignatius, a Philosopher by profession and obviously by inclination, had a fixation with England and all things English. He loved Churchill, was fascinated by the writings of Evelyn Waugh (no, he **didn't** think that she was a woman!), and even appreciated the humour of P G Wodehouse. He could, I felt, become the cornplaster that I didn't need: but he was kind, insisted on buying me a coffee, and then accompanied me to the village shop to stock up for breakfast, before he went to the service at the little church opposite the Refugio Gaucelmo for the Blessing of the Stones.

These were the stones that pilgrims would place on the pile at the foot of the Cruz de Ferro next day, I imagine.

I never saw him again until breakfast time.

I'd been carrying his breakfast about in a carrier bag all this time, and was worried that it might come down to handing them over to the Authorities with a brief description of the owner in case he should have – well, never mind, it all worked out fine in the end.

I'd originally wanted to stay at the Refugio Gaucelmo, because after all it is supported by our 'club', the Confraternity of St James, and it's nice to drop in to your own place, so to speak.

But when I'd arrived at 11.30, sweating buckets, and learnt from Bernard sitting smugly up there in pole position that it didn't open for three hours, the fleshpots won. But I did call in, Ignatius-free, and met the two cheery Wardens, midway through their two week stint: Trevor, and Maurice from Horley (which is just up the road from me).

He imagined that he might know my face. Well, it's possible, it's been around a long time.

It's a lovely cosy Refuge, dependant on donations: a contrast to the sleeker private Refuge where I had paid to rest my head.

He told me that the English Family On A Walking Holiday had stayed there a day or so earlier, arriving like drowned rats late in the evening after having sheltered ineffectively from the usual torrential afternoon rainstorm, sitting in a ditch beneath a sheet of polythene belonging to a Polish cyclist.

They'd been delighted to be all together on mattresses in the library: dried out and refreshed, they'd left in good spirits.

I also dropped in at the village shop to place a large order, a single yoghourt for breakfast. I don't know how it happened, but I spoke in English: and the lady replied in a Geordie accent. She'd spent a few months in Newcastle about ten years ago and couldn't speak highly enough about their warmth and kindness.

Her husband had been an English teacher (no, not an 'English' teacher, but a teacher of English if you want to be pedantic). He was working in the house across the street.

So I went over.

No, he wasn't poring over a computer screen: he was mixing cement.

Yes, he had taught English, and Maths and Economics as well, to students up to University Entrance level: now he was a bricklayer, and he found it much more satisfying.

You could see an end product, he said, which you couldn't with English although you could with Maths.

He was a happy philosopher: I doubt that Ignatius would have been at ease in his company.

I sauntered back for a meal at the Albergue del Pilar. It was full to the rafters: and the courtyard was packed with chattering pilgrims, getting stuck into their bar meals, inspecting each others feet, and getting worked up about The Big One, the climb to the Cruz de Ferro on Monte Irago at 1,504 m.

Pilgrims traditionally lay a stone in prayer on the huge pile at the foot of the Cruz de Ferro, which many had brought from their homes all over the world.

I had ham and eggs: two eggs and three deliciously grilled ham steaks, swimming in a sea of Poly Very Much Saturated Fat, mopped up with bread, and eased down with a glass of wine. It was magical!

Day 27

Rabanal del Camino to Riego de Ambrós

19 km   231 km to go

I decided to follow the old (real) Camino rather than the modern 'high' road.

Of course, the original Camino always went through the centre of the villages, as Trevor pointed out, because these had grown up alongside the road that the pilgrims walked: and although some sections had now been by-passed by modern roads, the old road and the old villages still survived.

Fortunately, there was a full moon at 06.00: and I was able to pick my way with care (no torch: take a good flashlight!) for those first two stony kilometres.

I was passed by a long striding lissom Spanish girl, who strode past as if I had been standing still: there are enormous numbers of these solitary lady pilgrims, eating up the miles with their sunburnt legs.

I was also passed by Jeremy the Japanese (his real name was too difficult to say, apparently).

He'd been sitting in the middle of the steep village street in Rabanal yesterday, doing a complex black and white sketch of the church: but nobody minded, and cars just made their way round.

I heard 'Ora!' ('Hola!' with a Japanese accent) at my elbow as he passed: and his blonde highlights and multicoloured headband rapidly vanished up the road into the breaking dawn.

It was a long, long drag up the asphalt road to the now abandoned village of Foncebadón. No, let's be fair, it's not **completely** abandoned: the guide book credits it with a population of two – in summer.

Only an expensive restaurant, and a Refuge beside the church, survived. Both were now closed.

I picked my way through the ruins of what had once been a thriving community, which had somehow eked out a subsistence living in this bleak windswept area of the mountains of northern Spain: but what a welcoming sight it must have been for pilgrims for almost a thousand years!

Another hard 1.5 km to the Cruz de Ferro, between rocky slopes clad with gnarled and twisted tree heathers and pines.

They'd resisted the temptation to build a snack bar at the top:

not even a mobile ice cream van. Good job, too.

The tiny iron cross, on top of an immense wooden tree trunk in the midst of a small mountain of stones, was the focal point for tens of thousands of pilgrims every year. I added my stone for Myfanwy, and prayed in meditation for a few minutes.

Of course, all we pilgrims photographed each other to the point of exhaustion. Soon we were all photographed-out.

The Cruz de Ferro surrounded by pilgrims' prayers

The guide book raved about 'the wonderful views all around'. Must have been an old guide book: you couldn't see anything through the dense woodland on either side of the long ridge until you were well down the hill towards El Acebo.

Ignatius kept popping up from behind trees and dilapidated huts, eager spectacles sparkling, asking 'Is everything alright, Harry?'

'Yes', I growled, 'It's OK'.

The ridge led down and then up – and then down **again**, to Manjarín, where I'd been hoping to get my daily 'fix'.

Manjarín. I once met a pilgrim who'd stayed there – for an hour!

No such luck! The only inhabited building amongst the piles of stones that had once been a village was a 'simple refuge, best described as atmospheric', a euphemism used by the guide books and run for many years by Tomás, who rings the bell as pilgrims approach.

When the authorities threatened to cut off his electricity supply, he'd gone on hunger strike on the steps of their offices in León unless they reconsidered: it was daylight when I visited, so there wasn't a light on anyway, and I couldn't tell if his campaign had been effective.

If you decide to say overnight, you can use the mattresses on the floor, the primitive toilet and the outdoor cooking facilities: I met a pilgrim who had opted to stay there, and he'd left after an hour.

A notice announced that Tomás (and his friends, who lurked deep within the Refuge) didn't sell food or drink: obviously no cappuccino machine lurked in the dark fastnesses of this collection of ramshackle sheds.

A big signpost, beneath a large Spanish flag, lists the distances to all the places that you might be on your way to visit, such as Machu Picchu or New York.

I got my *sello*, and made my donation.

It was quite an experience: I didn't meet anybody who walked past without a visit. Just past Manjarín, which lies in the shadow of a military radar station, you climb to the highest point on the Camino, at 1,517 m (4,950 ft). So you can see how bleak it is: and how glad a pilgrim trapped in one of the frequent storms must be to dash into the Refuge.

Seven kilometres down the calf straining descent to El Acebo, once I'd passed the Military Radar Station: now, that must have been (not) a great posting for a soldier. The final drop down the steep rocky trail to El Acebo was perilous: it was so sheer that you could imagine dropping a stone straight down the chimneys of the houses on the edge of the town without any particular effort.

A little way down the main street is the bar, which doubles as a Refuge.

El Acebo: downhill all the way

I'd decided to stop there: I was very tired.

Ignatius greeted me with a sycophantic smile.

I ate a crispy *empanada* with my café con leche grande whilst I waited to see if and when they were going to open: and if they did, whether or not they fancied me as a guest. The lady behind the bar appeared undecided, although she'd already checked in a couple of ladies who didn't look as if they would cause trouble.

I'd done my own little survey, as I'd pointed out to Ignatius the previous evening when we were being philosophical together, and I thought that it had the legs to become the subject for a really boring philosophical thesis in the hands of a committed PhD student. Namely, the further west we travel along the Camino, the smaller and more expensive a café con leche grande becomes.

He nodded thoughtfully, intrigued by the potential philosophical ramifications.

I sat on an old bench in the street outside, whilst the lady behind the bar considered my application to stay for the night.

I chatted with a party of Belgian cyclists. There were thirty in the group, said the leader, and they were 'doing' the Camino in seven days, 100 km plus every day.

Yesterday they'd 'done' 150 km. They'd be in Santiago two days later, 214 km away. The youngest was a boy of twelve; the group even included a lady who had never really ridden a bicycle before. I think she was the one who was getting on her bicycle rather gingerly, grimacing a little.

It was all obviously meant to be admirable: a Challenge with a tangible reward, destined for a frame on the wall. Well, it's all of those things: but there's actually a serious meaning behind the Challenge which might just be escaping them! Was it a commercial enterprise? I forgot to ask.

Anyway, I was getting a bit fed up waiting for the lady behind the bar to make up her mind: I got my *sello* and told Ignatius that I might as well carry on to Riego de Ambrós, only a couple of kilometres down the road.

He took my decision philosophically, as you would expect.

I doubted that my departure would affect the financial future of the Refuge at El Acebo. They were the most offhanded, dismissive almost surly Hospitaleros that I had met in all those long days: and their *empanada* was dried up as well!

I set off on the two kilometre descent: after having rested up for an hour or so, I felt a bit – well, not great.

The 40 bunk Refuge at Riego de Ambrós was new, purpose built; and the facilities and welcome were out of this world. It hadn't made it into the usual pilgrim guide books, though: and you had to keep your eyes open for the sign beside the road through the village.

I was greeted by a smiling young Hospitalero: relieved as well, I guess, because at 1.30 pm I was his first pilgrim of the day. He probably kept popping out to see if anybody had pinched the sign beside the road.

I sat and browsed through the Libro de Peregrinos, kept at every Refuge, in which pilgrims would write flattering remarks: those here seemed remarkably sincere, which cheered me up a lot. The Hospitalero seemed a bit down: so I wrote lots of nice things in the book to cheer him up.

Two lady pilgrims dropped in, used the toilets and set off for Molinaseca, 5 km down the valley. I tried to get them to stop, murmuring 'Es fantastica aquí' (which I meant to mean 'It's fantastic here'), but to no avail.

The Hospitalero announced that he was going for his lunch at 3.00 pm, as I was scrubbing my washing with a piece of Spanish carbolic that I'd found under the sink beneath the verandah.

I was effectively in charge! I didn't like to let him down by going out, as he was such a nice chap. He looked critically at the chromium plated staircase rail leading up to the dormitories, and gave it a final polish with his sleeve.

I didn't like to grip it and leave finger marks, so I kept well to the centre of the enormous slate steps.

Then he was gone.

How would I cope? I'll never know: nobody came.

The only downside at the Refuge was the plumbing system: whatever you did, the overflow from the (hot!) shower seeped out onto the floor. I bunged up the outlet in one of the plugless super deluxe stainless steel washbasins with a plug of toilet paper (it's alright, I cleaned it out when I'd finished!) to hold enough water for a shave, the first for five days.

It was so clinical, it looked like the sluice room in Casualty: but the basins were so inconveniently placed as to be disastrous, and leaked all over the simulated marble top and floor.

By now, I felt personally involved here: I was getting a guilt complex, as if it were **my** fault that the Refuge was empty. So I got the mop and bucket out and swabbed everywhere enthusiastically.

You slept in tiny two or four bunk cubicles, with sliding doors at each end: plump mattresses and thick pillows. I took the cubicle at the top of the stairs, just behind a little sitting area with a glass topped table and easy chairs and a small writing desk: it looked down over the lobby where the Hospitalero sat, looking as if he were suffering a bad dream. I just hoped that he wasn't on commission. He cheered up a bit when the last two pilgrims checked in at 6pm to bring the numbers up to three: yesterday, a party of cyclists had arrived just as it was getting dark, so there was hope yet. Mr Micawber would have been proud of him.

It was inexplicable, considering more than 100 pilgrims had packed the bar yesterday at Rabanal, a very convenient 19 km away over the Cruz de Ferro.

I wandered round the kitchen: split level, shaded, expensive wood topped work tops, and cupboards full of half empty packets and tins donated by long forgotten pilgrims. Most of them had probably been there since before sell by dates had been invented. I opened and shut every conceivable door, **but I couldn't find a stove.**

I was rather relieved, in a way, because cooking isn't really my thing. It's just that I thought that I should make an effort occasionally: and it cheered me up that I'd done so, and that **it wasn't my fault that I couldn't**.

The upmarket bar/restaurant down the road (I know it was upmarket, because it was called a 'mesón') served Pilgrim Meals *(menu peregrino, por favor?)*

Should be good, I imagined: trouble is, I didn't feel too good.

A heavy cold, caught from Andrew, the father in The English Family On A Walking Holiday, had dropped onto my chest. I prescribed myself a course of antibiotics, which I just happened to have in my enormous medical box for just such an eventuality.

As I'd thrown away the packet and instructions in the interests of space saving, I had to work out the dosage by counting up the tablets and dividing by seven (I had the idea that it was a seven day course, and when I divided 21 by seven it worked out at three, which seemed about right).

I began the course immediately, and soon felt **much** better!

But the meal was not so good: another Rule of the Camino, the more expensive a restaurant, the more secluded the corner reserved for pilgrims and the less impressive the meal.

That sounds terrible, as if I'm always whinging! I almost crossed it out: but I didn't.

Day 28

Riego de Ambrós to Ponferrada

13 km   212 km to go

I slept well in my cubicle: in fact, I didn't wake until 06.00 and even then I had to drag myself out of my bunk.

How to boil up the milk provided by the Hospitalero was a mystery to me, as I still couldn't find a stove or even a kettle. Even if I knew where he slept, I didn't think that he'd be happy if I shook him awake and said 'Sorry to bother you, but where's the stove?'

I hacked a bit off the hard flat loaf, ladled on cream cheese and jam, ate a sweet margarita cake, drank some milk and set off just after 07.00.

I strode down the main street, a song in my heart, but awash with guilt that I hadn't been away earlier. After 400 metres, an arrow led me to a narrow footpath, and – how glad I was that guilt hadn't dragged me from my bed earlier!

I searched my vocabulary for words to describe the path, and I still haven't come up with anything suitable.

It was mainly slates on edge, angled across the path and drawing you towards a sheer drop into the woods below, interspersed with big lumps that stretched for yards downhill at a steep angle and which must have made it suicidal in wet weather.

I edged my way downhill, trekking poles working overtime.

I lost count of the number of times I slipped and tripped. Well, that's a bit of an exaggeration, actually: it was eight: or was it nine? Anyway, it doesn't really matter.

There were a few quite nice stretches of several yards, which raised my spirits enormously: then it was back to shiny slippery slate.

Midway down the 5 km to Molinaseca was an enormous advertisement board, about two metres square, for a restaurant in the town. How they got it up there was a mystery to me: it must have come close to costing several lives.

I was busy taking a photograph of it when a voice hailed me: the first pilgrim of the day (as The Slowest Pilgrim, I was regularly passed by hundreds every day).

Suicide alley to Molinaseca

I looked up: it was Simian, the World's Greatest Snorer!

'Avanti!' he shouted, as he slithered past in a shower of rubble, miraculously staying upright as he did so, and vanished towards the valley below, where I could now look straight down the chimney pots of the slate roofed houses.

Half a kilometre from the road, I came across (wonders will never cease) a cast iron manhole cover. Perhaps it was above the main stream leading from the mountain spring that fed the town: and, should it get blocked (by a stray goat, for instance) they could rod it from there.

They'd obviously rodded it well recently, because the main street of Molinaseca was flooded. Water was several inches deep in the main street: street cleaners were trying to sweep it away with large brushes. They didn't appear to be making much progress. I went round it, and reached the last bar in town for my morning fix.

Now, here's another Pilgrim Tip.

I used the *servicios* (toilets to you): fortunately, I noticed the time clock controlled light switch outside the door of the *aseo* (sit downer). You can tell the time controlled switches: they have a little orange light inside them, so that you can find it if you panic in the dark when the light goes out.

Now, for some strange reason, these are often **outside** the door: you switch on and rush in. So, take my tip: take a torch in with you, because they are set to switch off quicker than any normal person has ever been know to complete his successful use of an *aseo*. Certainly, you couldn't take in the Daily Telegraph and spend a few minutes reading the report of Arsenal's latest match.

Because if you haven't got a torch, what do you do? No window, no light, door locked. You can either shuffle round the door with your shorts round your ankles, hoping that there is nobody outside, or if you speak fluent Spanish and you can hear somebody outside, shout 'Please turn on the light!' If he is naturally kindly, he will: if not, and he has a malicious sense of humour, he will go away or, even worse, stand quietly outside waiting for you to make the next move.

It was quite a nice walk out of Molinaseca, if you like walking along pavements beside main roads. I passed the municipal Refuge: lots of two tier bunks outside for *al fresco* sleeping in the hot summer.

My number one Guide Book suggested two routes: the first more scenic and slightly longer, the second largely beside a very busy road. Now, let me explain: 'scenic' is guide book speak for 'very hilly', whilst 'slightly longer' means double the distance of the easier, boring road option.

So when will I ever learn?

After the precipitous descent to Molinaseca, I should have welcomed an easier, boring option. But, it was nice up in the hills as I circled Ponferrada.

Ponferrada might be a heavily industrialised town, but the new Municipal Refuge is tremendous. I was number six in line, waiting for the one o'clock rush for the door where the Hospitalero and his friends were waiting to beat you off and subdue you into an orderly queue.

There was a large raised pond outside the main doors: and although you were sternly instructed to 'Keep off the grass' on a huge lawn surrounding a big statue, they didn't mind you sitting on the wall around the pond and dangling your battered feet in the water.

The wall was soon packed with footsore pilgrims: it could hold getting on for twenty at a time. It was a big pool, with a fountain in the middle, and comfortably warmed by the sun: a natural breeding ground for water borne foot infections.

The Hospitalero team took some time to get into their stride: they were all volunteers, and did brilliant work, and without them the Camino would grind to a halt within days.

'Where had I started?' asked the lady at the desk: information that had to be entered in their record book.

I pointed to the first *sello* on the front page: 'St Jean Pied de Port'.

She brightened up at this: she'd been going to put Riego de

Ambrós.

She was baffled as to what nationality to enter, until I pointed to 'England' in large letters on the front page of my Pilgrim Passport: but to be fair, that baffled almost everybody, everywhere. Now, 'Inglaterra' would have been different: they'd all heard of **that.** They usually settled for GB or UK.

Simian was number four in the queue: and, wonder of wonders, when we were allocated to our four-bunk rooms, we were in different rooms! Unless his room mates joined forces and ejected him into the corridor, I should be safe in the company of three lean cyclists.

The Refuge appeared to be a bottomless pit regarding numbers.

Pilgrims poured in all afternoon. Fortunately, the kitchen was underused: so I cooked my emergency litre of nourishing chicken soup into which I poured a very modest amount of left-over rice from the surplus-stock store on the shelf. It swelled up to enormous proportions: a litre of chicken-flavoured crunchy undercooked rice. None of the Cordon Bleu cooks knocking up amazing recipes wanted the remainder. I surreptitiously tipped the steadily swelling mass into the garbage bin, and hoped it wouldn't overflow into the kitchen

I asked one of the Hospitaleros if there was a *supermercado* or *autoservicio* nearby, so that I could replace my soup, and stock up for breakfast.

'It is August 15th,' she remarked, with a strong German accent: 'a holiday, so of course they are closed'.

She smiled with satisfaction as she imparted this potentially disastrous news.

Of course! How could I have forgotten? August 15th is a holiday to celebrate – well, I forget what, but as you can imagine, it was pretty disastrous!

All I had was the hard quarter of a two day old baguette, some cream cheese segments, and a few of Francesc's biscuits from León.

Plus, as the German Accented Hospitalero pointed out helpfully, the leftovers in the fridge and on the shelves. Perhaps, after all, I was saved.

Trouble is, it's difficult to differentiate between 'dumped' or 'donated' food, and food which is being saved by pilgrims for their own use: I came across a guilty looking pilgrim in mid-bite, halfway through a pie, confronted by an angry would be eater who'd been looking forward to this particular nourishing item which he'd been storing carefully in the fridge to ward off night starvation.

It was a nasty moment: I don't like to imagine blood being spilt.

But even this was settled amicably: I never ever saw an example of Pilgrim Rage. I was thinking of my breakfast, I pointed out.

'Ah well, then you have no problems. All the shops will be open in the morning', and she smiled as she went off to round up a few more pilgrims.

I don't know what time she thought I got up: perhaps 08.00, leisurely shower, stroll down to the shops, breakfast at 09.00 and a mid-morning start.

By mid-morning, I hoped to be halfway to Villafranco del Bierzo.

She was right: all the shops were closed.

I walked round the pedestrianised centre of the town, past the castle and a house held up by a huge Wisteria. The Pilgrim Information Centre was closed for siesta, but I bought some postcards from a shop across the road. You have to buy your stamps from a 'tabac', though: sometimes you found a tabac which sold both stamps **and** cards, and then you were quids in, especially if there was a big yellow postbox nearby.

I found a restaurant, which from the outside looked like a London Gentleman's Club: there was a pilgrim room at the back, and I got a marvellous meal with the lady in charge pampering pilgrims shamelessly. She slipped me a few margarita cakes on the side. Great to be wanted.

It began to spot with rain as I strolled back to the Refuge: I broke into a shambling run, something impossible a fortnight ago. New pilgrims looked on enviously. I was wandering zombie-like round the kitchen when I heard a familiar 'Hel-**lo**!': and there was the smiling face of Francesc, who'd made a forced march after his day off at León visiting his grandma and seeing the Gloucester Girls off to England. 'How are **you**?'

I was able to reassure him: he appeared pleased, and went off to make himself a complicated cheese bocadillo with the aid of his Swiss-army knife.

I had a long chat with a Swiss Hospitalero volunteer: we philosophised about what the Camino had become. Ignatius would have been proud.

Yes, for many it was a deeply religious and spiritual experience, but for others an athletic or personal challenge with a big back-up safety-net.

The latter group seemed to be diminishing as the holiday period ended: Ponferrada, for instance, had welcomed 275 pilgrims a day only a week previously and today it was down to 170.

The one thing with which he couldn't come to terms were those who 'did the Camino' by car, one day on, one day off, the 'Camion camineros': and it wasn't even overt, it was quite obvious at times, with rucksacks being unloaded from cars directly outside the Refuge.

It was 10.30 pm when I got to bed: not such a problem, as the Swiss Hospitalero had made it clear that he wouldn't open the gates until 06.00.

Day 29

Ponferrada to Villafranca del Bierzo

21 km   199 km to go

I woke up just after 1.00 pm: I could hear the laboured breathing of Simian, the Worlds Greatest Snorer, way down the corridor. Less than 200 km to go to Santiago, I thought gleefully: but hang on a minute, that's another ten days!

By five o'clock, I'd worried myself enough to get up. The kitchen was awash with frustrated pilgrims, who hadn't been able to force the gates or storm the high wall. Tensions were building!

The guard relented at 05.51, and a seething mass of pilgrims made for the Camino, with Simian and his friend up front. They'd soon built up a commanding lead.

The first kilometre was brilliant: yellow arrows at every turn. Just enough to get you out of the centre of town: then, at a large traffic island with four equal exits, zilch!

Pilgrims were milling round: the leader, white haired Simon with his knee bandage fluorescing in the half light (Simian and his friend were long gone, they must have known something we didn't), was called back to harangue a street sweeper and two lads returning from a heavy night-out, whose information might not have been totally accurate.

In the end a chap coming out of a block of flats informed us that Simon, after all, had probably been right.

He seemed a trifle annoyed and shot off up the road, the point of his stick tap-tapping the pavement angrily. I was a close second, until I was overtaken by a young couple. The girl had been infected by the epidemic of red hair: no wonder they were moving fast.

A couple of portly middle-aged Spaniards, Juan and Pedro, were hard on their heels. We sped for six kilometres through the unlovely built-up suburbs of Columbrianos and Fuentesnuevas: at Camponaraya, a plump (that's fatter than portly, by the way) German shot out of a side street, carrying his breakfast in a supermarket bag, and tagged on at my elbow. I was in danger of losing touch with the leaders, in sixth place.

Pedro was beginning to labour under the pressure, and was coming back to me fast. Juan was looking back at him anxiously over his shoulder: team medals looked in danger.

We crossed the road: and suddenly the young couple had been replaced by a middle aged pair. How had this happened?

I was up to fourth when Juan and Pedro stopped for a drink: but they soon came back up the field, working as a pair, and took me at the corner of a building site, whilst the Plump German With His Breakfast In A Supermarket Carrier Bag overtook us all and shot into fourth place.

Nine kilometres gone in only an hour and a half, and Simon was just a shock of white hair and a fluorescent knee bandage in the distance.

You couldn't even hear the tapping of his stick.

Still no yellow arrows *(flechas)*: I daren't even stop for a drink.

Then we came to a motorway junction, crossed an underpass, and into an area of neglected vines and woodland, and we all sort of lost interest.

Simon obviously took the gold medal: the rest of us couldn't care less who came second and third.

Four kilometres to Cacabelos, where a huge roadside sign informed us that the town welcomed pilgrims, and that the 13 bars and 8 restaurants were there only to serve.

It's a bit of an upmarket town: and at 08.42, with a big festival planned for later in the day, it didn't appear to want a mass of sweaty pilgrims infesting their restaurants and bars. They solved the problem by remaining closed until we'd gone, and the danger of infection had passed.

Pity. I'd been looking forward to my café con leche grande.

A lady was setting out tables and chairs in front of one of the bars: when I asked if she was open, she snapped 'Cerrado (closed)' and slammed the door, peering though the window until she was sure I'd gone.

I sat on the wall of an enormous mediaeval wine press just outside town, which looked man enough to have crushed enough grapes to supply all the wine bars of Outer London for a year, and ate my breakfast.

Four elegant 'pilgrims' were posing for their video cameras outside the motel-style Cacabelos Pilgrim Refuge, with it's twin bedded rooms (that's according to one of my guidebooks, can't vouch for it personally, but they don't usually publish duff information so it's probably correct).

They were getting ready to walk **all the way to Villafranca!** Must have been all of 9 km!

Gleaming shoes, shorts with razor sharp creases, socks sparkling, shirts untainted by sweat: and on his head, one had a jaunty straw hat. Two of them carried very small daysacks: the others were without.

They were snapping at my heels over the next 5 km beside

the highway, stopping only to video an uninspiring view of distant Villafranca del Bierzo.

I lost them over the last four kilometres over dusty tracks through the vineyards, which started off wide enough to take a jeep, and ended with my wondering if by some chance I'd lost the way, it was so narrow: until I reached a few isolated houses and a good stony road leading down to the town.

The Municipal Refuge was the first building that you met on the edge of town, just below the road: Simian and his friend were already waiting beside the door.

Almost opposite was the 15th century Romanesque church, the Iglesias Santiago, where pilgrims who were unable to continue any further received at the Puerta del Perdón (the door of forgiveness), by Papal Decree, the same privileges that they'd have received as if they'd reached Santiago, same (I think) as the Alto de Perdón.

Sadly, all the time that I was there, the door was shut and nobody came: I must find out what my entitlements would have been, it might be useful.

I went inside and said a few prayers: then I carried on for a few yards to have a look at the 'legendary' Refugio Fenix, built by and for pilgrims by the famed Jesús Jato.

Julian, who I'd met at Ponferrada, came out of the door. He'd walked the Camino several times: and Refugio Fenix, he implied, had not improved over the past two or three years and no longer had the warm welcoming atmosphere that he remembered.

A fire hadn't improved the ambience, either: one half was shrouded in polythene sheeting, the rest looked like an old railway carriage.

But I loved the look of it, and wandered round inside (as you can, in Refuges, it's open house to pilgrims), and still wish now that I'd stayed there, it is such a legend along the Camino. So is Manjarín: but at no time did I wish I'd stayed **there!**

Julian, who looked as if he should be sporting a cravat and a billycock hat, wandered off down into Villafranca with his lissom, suntanned companion.

I checked in at the Municipal Refuge: clean, sterile, comfortable and well worth €3 for the night. Yes, I know that I could have changed my mind and gone back to the Refugio Fenix: and to my constant regret, I didn't!

Front of the queue was – Simian!

Once again, I was in the next bunk: his snoring equipment was flexed and at the ready. Francesc also arrived. He'd texted Julia and Rachel, the Gloucester Girls, who seemed pleased to hear that we'd all met up again.

I strolled down town.

The shaded side of the enormous square in the centre of Villafranca was crowded with tables and chairs, shaded by advertising umbrellas, in front of the bars and restaurants. The town policeman, immaculate in helmet, heavy uniform and white gloves, was perspiring heavily as he courteously guided the one-way traffic through a complex chicane between the tables and chairs.

It was Saturday: early closing was imminent.

I went to the Supermarket, to buy the raw materials for breakfast. It was packed with pilgrims, fighting it out with determined local matrons, all aware that it closed in half an hour at 2 pm.

The girl at the only check out open seemed to take it all in her stride: the old man at her side (about my age, actually) packed the bags imperturbably.

I was 15th in the queue: the line stretched far beyond me,

right back to the meat counter against the back wall.

They coped, as they always had.

Soon I was sitting outside on a bench, sipping a Fanta Limón and eating a bar of white chocolate. Then I sauntered over to the restaurants.

Empanada? No, they had none.

Tortilla? Bit heavy.

Pizza? Seemed not quite right in Spain: like the restaurant in Mid-Sussex advertising 'English Food: kebabs, pizza, fish and chips'.

As usual when I can't make up my mind, I settled for fried eggs, bacon and chips with a glass of cider.

I felt inexplicably tired as I dragged myself up the steep hill to the Refuge, and a two hour siesta.

I cooked some nourishing mushroom soup for supper, with bits of pasta thrown in and the end of tomorrow's loaf: two young Germans gave me a piece of melon.

Francesc did amazing things to half a dozen carrots with his Swiss Army knife.

The kitchen made any sort of cooking an adventure, with most of the equipment plastered with notices indicating that it would be unwise to use it. Happily, we all survived.

Simian, having surveyed me silently for the past five days, informed me that his name was Rafael, and that the plump friend by his side was named Antonio.

I told him that my name was Harry.

We all seemed much better for this exchange of information.

Day 30

Villafranca del Bierzo to Ruitelán

18 km   **178 km to go**

I slept in: in fact, didn't even stir until 05.30. The dormitory was still pulsating to the steady throb of Simian's energetic snoring tackle.

I left at 06.45. Simian was still snoring. Should I wake him? Better not.

A butch pilgrim, with a seven day beard and a ragged moustache and who bore a startling resemblance to one of the more aggressive French rugby props preparing to outstare Martin Johnson, was posturing and flexing his muscles before a group of (possibly) admiring ladies, patting children on the head and offering round spare food.

I won't mention his name in case he reads this and decides to give up Martin Johnson and go for something easier.

As for the Camino, I was faced with an embarrassment of riches: a choice of three routes!

These were

a) a (very slightly longer, which means double the distance of the next route listed) high level route,

b) a low level one and

c) a longer, strenuous option via Dragonte.

This last, apparently, had been the route used by pilgrims in the past who were either ill, or with infectious diseases. There was a monastery up there, at Villar de Corrales, which had a spring with healing properties. Good job, bearing in mind the health of their clientele.

One of my guide books noted that, apart from being 13 km

longer, this particular route is now 'overgrown and blocked by trees in places' and that a little further on, you have to negotiate a huge opencast quarry, shortly after which you reach a signpost which points in exactly the wrong way. Route finding, the guide book notes, has become difficult, and there are no facilities except fountains.

It ends 'All in all, this route is no longer recommended'.

I should think that it significantly reduced the numbers of sick pilgrims, as well.

I followed a group of lady pilgrims through the town, who had suddenly popped out of the door of a Hostal: they looked as though they might favour b).

It took such a long time to get on to the open road that I thought I must have gone round the town twice, especially as the limited supply of available *flechas* (arrows) soon ran out. The lady pilgrims had a guide with them (they were probably on a Pilgrim Package Tour), so I felt safe and tucked in behind at a reasonable distance.

The guide left. We were on our own.

It was quite nice beside the main road, especially when we were protected behind a high concrete barrier: it reminded me of the A23 at Pease Pottage, where the motorway traffic hadn't quite come to terms with the narrower roads and the novel idea of reduced speed.

There were a couple of quiet detours through tiny hillside villages, where time was standing increasingly less still. I caught up with a heavyweight pilgrim in Pereje, wearing an enormous rucksack and pulling his wife's backpack on a luggage trolley.

His wife had her hands full towing the dog along on it's lead. I stopped for breakfast at the Motorway Café just outside Trabadelo, which gave more attention to food than souvenirs.

On the way to Ruitelán

Wish they could do the same in England.

Pringles, dried up *empanada*, bar of chocolate, banana and a café con leche went down well: I sat with the two young Germans, Matthias and Tobias (you **know**, the ones who'd given me some melon last night!): they'd inadvertently taken the 'scenic route' over the mountain. Not, I guess, via Dragonte or they'd probably still be wandering round up there.

Why were **they** walking the Camino?

It was, said Matthias, the sense of peace and freedom: at home, if someone damaged his motorbike, for instance, he felt anger. It was all put into perspective on the Camino. We all had enough for our needs.

They finished my Pringles and left.

I sauntered through ancient chestnut woods, where there was not a sound to disturb the silence, sunlight slanting through the branches onto the track: then it was back to reality through

Trabadelo and the obligatory photograph in heroic pose in front of the fountain, and into Ambasmestos along a road with the imaginative name of CALLE CARRETERA NATIONAL VI.

Bit like saying you lived in Ml ROAD in England.

But there was no doubt that it was factually correct, and it certainly got the message over. No problem for the postman, either.

I'd decided to stop at the Refuge at Vega de Valcarce: but I couldn't find it. As my guide book noted that it is 'reported basic, cold water, no kitchen', I wasn't too bothered. But perhaps it's better now: I met pilgrims later who'd stayed there and survived.

I carried on up the steep road for a further 2 km to Ruitelán. I was now in Galicia!

160 km to Santiago! My first step tomorrow would bring the distance below 100 miles!

I was first there at 13.00: until 15.00, I thought that perhaps I'd done a Riego de Ambrós. It was the most welcoming Refuge that I was ever to meet. The Hospitalero and his wife and the extended family group and friends that lived there were all smiley, some spoke English, but all went out of their way to help: and amazingly, you only paid on leaving, in case you were unhappy with the welcome you'd received!

The entrance hall was plastered with postcards from satisfied pilgrims, and I'm not surprised!

An Unhappy Lady Vegan arrived, trailing clouds of discontent. Life had dealt her a rough hand was her message: and she was determined to share it with everybody else. Then came a group of eleven German pilgrims, led by a Jesuit Pastor, and recruited from every corner of Germany via the internet.

The showers weren't just warm, they were HOT; and the two little dormitories had a cosy intimate feel. I hurried to do my washing: as usual, when I've got lots of time, I waste it and suddenly find myself playing catch-up. Clothes lines hung above the rocky slab that passed for the back garden; it was literally 'a house built upon a rock', and high above the road which you reached by a flight of steep steps.

Ruitelán might just be a blur, in a fast car: but it is a perfect microcosm of a Spain that is now, sadly, rapidly disappearing. I peered into a dark cowshed, sweet with the smell of cattle, on the main street with old uneven houses touching on either side: a bar that was the centre of village life, with patrons sitting on uneven chairs almost on the road itself; a Refuge where the Hospitalero radiated happiness and welcome: and the little church, a low plain building with *Iglesias* (church) picked out in stones on it's wall beside the road, just in case you should be in any doubt.

It was Sunday, and the Jesuit Pastor held a simple and very moving service in the almost primitive little church.

The Hospitalero provided a meal for those who wished

Inside the lovely little church at Ruitelán

(everyone) around the kitchen table. Thirteen of us pilgrims: it was like a big happy family meal that included the extended family of the Hospitalero.

Wine and bread, home made *gazpacho*, salad with fish and cheese, and an egg custard.

Everybody shared: everybody gained.

Even the telephone joined in the celebrations: I must have got ten minutes for €2 ringing England to speak with our eldest two sons Mark and Stewart. I was so sorry to miss Stewart and Krysta's visit from the USA, with their children, but it was nice to speak with Mark, Lucy, William, Ronan and Alice.

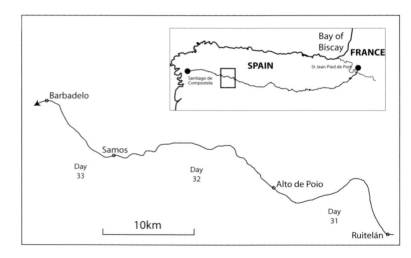

10

Over O Cebreiro into Green Galicia

Day 31

Ruitelán to Alto de Poio

17.5 km   160 km to go

Nobody snored that night in our eight bed dormitory, unless I did (did I detect a certain coolness next morning when we woke?)

The Hospitalero woke the sleeping Refuge (yes, nobody tried to leave early!) with music piped direct to the dormitories: Ave Maria, followed by The Three Tenors.

Decibel levels were high.

Breakfast again was communal: toast, honey, jam and butter, bowls of chocolate or coffee, fruit, margaritas unlimited: it was a really jolly event.

I'd ditched the unopened 1.5 litre bottle of water, which I'd been carrying for days as an extra insurance policy together with my packet of soup, bearing in mind that up ahead we faced the 'dreaded' climb over O Cebreiro!

What a difference it made!

I'd packed the night before and hastened for the door at 06.30. I thought that I detected the Unhappy Lady Vegan at the far end of the corridor, rucksack at the ready. As the Pastor remarked later at Alto de Poio, involvement would have meant becoming a part of her private unhappiness: and anyway, I like to walk alone.

I hurried up the road out of Ruitelán, pursued by the tapping of a stick. I was afraid to turn round, and I was relieved to be passed by a portly pilgrim sporting a natty bandana.

Down into the village of Herrerias: dawn began to break as I slowly tapped my way between the sleeping houses and up along the rough road towards O Cebreiro which had loomed forbiddingly over us last night (and for the entire previous week as well!).

I was blissfully unaware of what was to come.

O Cebreiro was only 1,300 m (just over 4,200 ft): but in those 9 km from Ruitelán, it meant a climb of 650 m (more than 2,100 ft), and there was the odd downhill in that as well to boost the average gradient!

But I was rapidly learning 'guide book-speak': and where it said ' a clear rocky track then zigzags it's way steeply uphill through chestnut woods to the village of La Faba', it really meant 'two kilometres of very strenuous track where crampons would be an asset'.

And yet: this had been the road that had kept these little villages and houses together since time immemorial, trodden by generations of people and their cattle and horses, and flanked by dry stone walls built painstakingly over the centuries.

Wooden logs were inserted across the way from place to place to steady the footing in the mud of winter. Occasionally gaps in the bank gave onto steep meadows, lush with grass, where cattle were grazing.

Chestnut woods had provided food and timber, and land for pigs to grub.

Rain was a constant companion.

As I thought about this, plodding my way up the steep hill, it began to come to life.

Life must have been unimaginably hard, even within living memory, in these bleak Galician hill villages.

At La Faba, pilgrims were offered the chance of Oriental Massages and Infusions by Marcelino, an unkempt gentleman reclining on two red upholstered railway carriage seats in front of his barn. His horse was tethered up the road, having a good nourishing breakfast. The price seemed reasonable, and could have included hand and foot massage, but as I was in a hurry, I declined the opportunity.

I asked if I could photograph him: he turned down this chance of immortality, and hurried inside the barn.

It didn't really matter: I think that I'd already photographed him from a distance, anyway, but I didn't like to tell him in case he got angry, and being chased by an angry hippy in the wilds of Galicia is not something that any pilgrim wants to contemplate.

Two more kilometres on a steep rocky track to Laguna de Castilla: I hurried for a drink from the fountain, which I thought was engraved 1562. But it was rather moss encrusted, and on closer inspection turned out to be 1962, which (historically speaking) was quite disappointing.

The marker stones, placed every half kilometre all the way to Santiago, began just outside the village at 153.Well, they ran **almost** all the way: they finished about 12 km from the end, but more about that later.

I loved them: I searched for them eagerly. I felt that I could count down now to the finish. If ever I get on 'Who Wants to be a Millionaire?', and the £1 million question is 'How far from Santiago do the half kilometre markers begin?' I'd get it **right**! I'd be a millionaire!

Actually, I missed the first two: but it wasn't really a big thing, and I didn't feel any compulsion to retrace my steps to find the missing two. Wait a minute, though … perhaps next year I could get a cheap flight to León, then a train, and perhaps a bus: bit of a walk, and … no, I **mustn't** get these thoughts!

The path became smoother as I climbed: the magical views all around tantalisingly emerged for just a few seconds at a time before the mist swirled over once again. A long high wall, built with bricks

Kilometre markers along the Camino, with pilgrim prayers on top

and mortar, and then I reached the summit of O Cebreiro.

It was strangely disappointing: what an anticlimax!

No trumpets, no fanfare, no big plaque proclaiming the fact beside which I could be photographed for posterity (I'm very big on posterity!): not even a Mr Whippy van, although it was now well past 09.00.

The trees around the parking area at the top hid any views, even if there had been no mist: and so I trudged a couple of hundred yards down to Mesón Anton to get the most enormous serve-your-own *sello* that I had yet encountered, and a cup of café con leche grande.

A couple of guys from the extended family at Ruitelán were standing on the viewpoint in the middle of this tiny village which was dedicated almost exclusively to helping pilgrims and day trippers unload their money for food and souvenirs. They'd turned up there because they just fancied an early morning stroll, and were going to stroll back again for lunch, probably to chop up the vegetables ready for the evening rush.

I finally broke, and got myself photographed by one of them standing with the other, against a steadily less misty background. Then off towards my target for tonight, the Refuge at Hospital de Condesa.

I picked up a few (small!) souvenir stones from the hillside, as the previous ones had been junked when they were mixed into a slurry with soggy plasters and toilet paper in the bottom of my waterlogged rucksack.

The road went up and down along the crest of the long ridge and over the Alto de San Roque, where I came across a young German lady cyclist beside the enormous statue of St James making giant strides to Santiago.

She'd once been on a school exchange visit to Broxbourne and Hoddesden in Hertfordshire: she cheered up when I told her that I knew them well. Actually, I'd probably been through there once when I worked at St Albans. We photographed each other, and felt much better.

The track led down away from the main road, into fragrant valleys and hillsides full of artemisia and rue, dianthus and cornflowers: it was my first taste of the 'green lanes' of Galicia. It took me past deserted tumbledown houses, up steep climbs, down rutted tracks, and finally along a minor road to Hospital de Condesa.

It was milking time: enormous placid brown cows, accompanied by equally docile dogs and even more docile old ladies in smocks and green wellies, were wandering along the road and segregating into their own stall in their own cowshed without need for direction, as they did day after day.

The Refuge, tucked away at the back of the farmyard, was

closed until 13.00: an hour and a half away. There was nothing else in the village except a tap. The stark Refuge didn't look too appealing, anyway (although I'm sure that, inside, it was probably sheer luxury, don't want to condemn anywhere sight unseen).

I sat down and knocked up a quick bocadillo from the oddments buried deep in my rucksack. Nothing much happened in the next five minutes. A gentleman sitting on his doorstep told me that the nearest bar, **which was also a Refuge** (I didn't know this, important information, which wasn't on most lists!) was 3 km away at Alto de Poio which at 1,337 m was the highest and furthest point along the ridge. So it would be all downhill from there, I worked out (well, that's the theory, anyway).

Rather than sitting beside the village tap watching the local slate cleaver in action for a couple of hours (fascinating, but could become a bit boring: didn't seem like a spectator sport), I set off along the ups and downs towards the Alto de Poio, following the marker stones and yellow arrows and counting down the steps (about 1,200 for every half kilometre, might sound boring, but I had to keep my mind active).

Half a kilometre from my objective, as I was standing photographing a graveyard in which families were stacked in their own personal chests of drawers round the walls, I got a nasty shock.

Could have given me a heart attack if I'd been in a weaker state, but as I'd just got O Cebreiro under my belt I felt remarkably robust.

A gentleman coming out of his farmyard with half a tree balanced on his shoulder informed me that, no, there was no Refuge at the bar at the top of the incredibly steep hill with which I was faced.

The nearest Refuge, he said, was at Triacastela, which I

The Alto de Poio is at the top! Well worth the climb!

worked out was 12.5 km further on.

But it all ended happily.

There **was** a Refuge at Alto de Poio: 19 places, plus an enormous table that could probably take (at a glance) a further six. There was also a pile of rough looking mattresses.

The young lady behind the bar noted down my name: she obviously had to keep records, so she scrawled 'Harry' on a piece of paper. Admission was by donation: she brightened up when I tendered €5, and even more when I gave her a 50 cents tip for my café con leche grande and a tin of Fanta Limón.

Her assistant sighed when I ordered a cheese bocadillo, and raised her eyes in silent supplication, before going off to the kitchen to produce the most inedible concoction of which it has ever been my misfortune to leave half.

But I grabbed the best bunk, a single between the washroom and the door, and sat outside admiring the most incredible view unfolding all around as the mist cleared. It's the sort that I had imagined when friends back home had said 'I bet you'll get some great photographs up there in the mountains'.

Far away, I could see the valleys stretching way beyond O Cebreiro to the east at the beginning of the ridge: and if I walked just a few yards round the front of the Refuge, I got the same view over Triacastela and beyond Samos, more than 20 km away in the distance to the west. If I'd sat on the roof, I'd have been able to see both at the same time, although of course it would have meant turning my head round a bit.

I hung my washing on a long line in the garden of an apparently deserted white house just up the hill. Nobody appeared to mind. Most of the other pilgrims did the same.

Nothing much happened for a couple of hours. I sat toying with my drink, watching boiled pilgrims emerging from the depths of the 'green lane' at the end of the car park.

They seemed pleased to reach the bar: hardly any realised there was a Refuge there. It avoided being overbooked by not giving anything away, such as writing 'Albergue' in big letters on the wall. News seemed to spread purely by word of mouth.

The Jesuit group arrived, in very good shape.

After they'd eaten, they held a democratic group meeting. This is usually a bad idea, as it generally deteriorates into an ill-tempered shouting match.

They decided to stop after a further 6 km, halfway to Triacastela, to sleep at a Hostal: and they even rang up to confirm it, something of which I'd never have thought. I'd have just hurried on and hoped for the best: it just showed how well organised they were.

The pastor organised similar pilgrimages every year: he was a super guy, and had a very nice group with him. Apparently, they held 'familiarisation' weekends in Germany before they left, at which the more obviously unsuitable were gently eased out: and it worked!

Interested in joining him next year? Sorry, I forgot to find out the website. Never mind, eh?

Yes, he thought that the Unhappy Lady Vegan was some distance behind: he also had been a little worried about her.

It was getting very hot: the Pastor and his team set off, and I retired to my bunk for a couple of hours of quality sleeping.

6.31: washing was dry (well, almost: good enough to wear, anyway). It was getting a bit cool at 4,345 ft and I might even need to grab one of the dirty blankets stacked in the lobby.

I crossed the road to the upmarket sounding Hotel Restaurant Santa Maria de Poio: this, apart from the dilapidated white house behind the pub where we all hung our washing, was the only other building in the village.

I waited patiently for several minutes whilst the lady behind the bar attended to her persistent heavy cold and chatted with the only other customer: in the end, I got the message and left. She didn't appear to mind. I'd already learnt that, in Spain, time stands still. Waiting is an art, ignoring is a test of character, and she was a **really** good ignorer.

How did she know I was still there, with her back turned? Could she see me in a mirror? Was the other customer giving her little hand signals indicating 'Don't turn round, he's still there'?

I'll never know. I don't think I'll ever become a good Spaniard.

It was back to the bar: the biggest greasy spoon that I've ever met in Spain.

The young lady sighed even more heavily when I ordered a Pilgrim Menu.

She threw down fork, knife and serviette with unerring accuracy.

She had the potential to make some man spectacularly unhappy for many years.

I could see into the kitchen through the open door behind the bar: she and an old lady in a dirty apron were conferring.

The macaroni was cool and greasy: the meat was fat and equally greasy, lamb garnished with boiled potatoes and sliced peppers. It was all nicely cool, so that there was no danger of my burning my mouth with the first hungry bite. The ice cream was the best bit: only because it was still sealed in it's carton.

The wine bottle was, of course, uncorked: no label, and covered with dirty fingerprints. But I like a good, rough full bodied red: I drank quite a lot, to help me to forget. Forget what? I forget.

It was the worst €4 three course meal that I've ever half eaten.

I didn't need that extra blanket, though. In fact, I really didn't need a sleeping bag at all, it was so hot in the dormitory.

Two young Swedes discovered what they suggested was a two way mirror (shades of James Bond!) set into the wall in the toilet/shower/wash room. We tried to work out where might be the other side: we were tempted to delay departure next day until mid-morning to see if we could buy a copy of any video behind the bar. Perhaps they saved them all up for winter viewing: after all, there can't be much to do on the Alto de Poio during those long winter nights.

Day 32
Alto de Poio to Samos
21.5 km   142.5 km to go

People got up reluctantly. I ate the remains of my two day old bocadillo from Villafranca, smeared with cream cheese, and it still tasted better than the one I'd bought here at the Alto de Poio yesterday.

Now, let me put the record straight. Reading through what I've written, you'd think that the Refuge at Alto de Poio was hell on earth. Well, it isn't: the dormitory is super comfortable and warm, with nice bunks: all I'd say is, bring your own pre-cooked food.

But I'd been in a bit of a dilemma as to whether to go to Sarria direct, or via Samos.

This was the main topic of discussion between us pilgrims the night before: there's not much night life in the more isolated Refuges and so we get our pleasures fleetingly.

A report that we found lying in the dormitory indicated that Samos was the nearest to Paradise on the Camino that one could find. 8 toilets, 8 showers, 80 luxury bunks, washing and drying machines.

That settled it for me. I couldn't cover the twenty one and a half kilometres quickly enough.

Yesterday had been magical: the climb to O Cebreiro and the panoramic views that had opened along the ridge culminating in the all-round vista from the Alto de Poio after several kilometres of the lovely Galician 'green lanes', sunken lanes between the tiny green fields. Steep, yes: but magical none the less.

Today promised to be similar.

I retrieved the battered straw hat that I'd thrown into the skip yesterday and dusted off the bits of rejected food sticking to it (and there's plenty of **that** at the Alto de Poio!).

Two kilometres down the road, I got a stone in my shoe: the first in more than 600 km.

I sat, one shoe off, one shoe on, doing the necessary.

A couple passed. 'Ah, mosquitoes' remarked the lady.

First view of the monastery at Samos

It was misty all the way to Triacastela, 12 km deprived of what I knew to be beautiful views but with only the mountain tops peeping out above the clouds: and from Triacastela, after a further couple of kilometres, it was back into the green lanes all the way to the Monastery at Samos.

As they say, 'What comes up, must go down': pretty shrewd, eh?

Because the green lanes aren't content to meander alongside the river: they cross it many times, but always at the bottom of a steep descent and before an even steeper climb. I'm basically a coward: and I dreaded the prospect of what the guide book called 'a very steep descent'. In fact, it should have read 'a very very steep descent': and just when I'd got over picking my way gingerly down the slippery dusty loose stones, I was faced with something infinitely more challenging the other side of the bridge.

But at the top, after I'd crossed the road, the full majesty of the enormous Monastery at Samos was revealed far below.

Once, it had housed 500 monks: now only 18 remained (no, not from the original 500: they'd be pretty old by now, and I'd be very surprised if even one remained, let alone 18. They'd be about 600 years old. These were recent monks!). I didn't take the guided tour: but a pilgrim who had, told me of the luxurious settings amidst which they lived their very simple lives.

When I got there and joined the queue outside the Refuge, I found that the truth didn't live up to our expectations.

I wish the report that I'd read had been there now, so that I could have ceremoniously torn it up.

There were only four unisex toilets and showers (from very cool to cold), certainly no special washing facilities (you just had to monopolise the wash basins), and nowhere to hang your clothes to dry except on some lines between the street trees or fixed to the wall above where the public sat, on the other side of the main road. Be careful when you cross the road, as well!

Oh yes, there's no kitchen either; and the restaurant across the road was shut today! I could go on, but I won't: it would only be churlish because, after all, it's clean, there's a roof over our

You've still got to hang your washing on the other side of the road!

heads, a bunk with a mattress on which to lie, and shelter: and without these, we'd be lost. There's plenty of restaurants around: and after all, we're pilgrims anyway and everybody got on with it cheerfully.

Just thought I'd mention it, though, in case you can't decide between Samos and Sarria (that's an extra 7 km, by the way, on a different road from Triacastela).

I just wish that I had the time, like Thomas, The Old Irish Man With The Long White Beard Who Spent The Winter At Fatima In Portugal who I met later, to walk every possible alternative route along the Camino rather than hustling along in a straight line, focused on finding a bunk on which to get my head down that night.

Now, I'd not yet come across an example of 'Pilgrim Rage', but we nearly got it today. Sorry about that.

I was fourth in the queue, eager to lay my hands on an old iron bedstead and squashed mattress in pole position, when along came a pugnacious gentleman, who looked startlingly like Timothy Bull, with a clip board marshalling twenty or so youngsters and adults all wearing T shirts proclaiming 'Diabeticos en el Camino'.

An aggressive lady and her sheepish husband took the opportunity to squeeze in with them ('Bring the bags, John', but in French, you know I'm multilingual).

Now I'm all for fundraising: but when they push their way to the front and grab the prime block of twenty bunks around the washrooms, it's time to make your feelings known in the most firm (but gentlemanly: after all, I **am** English) way possible! Such as saying to the awfully nice young English speaking German volunteer at the desk 'I was fourth in the queue, and now I'm twenty fourth'.

The Spanish Hospitalero had by now thrown in the towel, or

more accurately the Pilgrim Passports, which he slammed down on the desk. He wandered away with his hands clamped between his legs, in a sort of defensive standing foetal position. I thought he was going to burst into tears.

I outstared Timothy Bull, who protected the group of young Diabeticos en el Camino behind his outstretched arms, and jostled one of his helpers (in a gentlemanly way, of course, although I don't think that I said 'Sorry').

When I was allocated a lower bunk in a prime position close to the door by the young German helper, an international incident was narrowly averted.

But I was glad to hear that the pugnacious Leader Of The Diabeticos En El Camino had got up the noses of both the young German and his tearful Spanish boss. Monks, one felt, don't behave like that!

And so we were all happy ever after: and I went off to the Supermarket to buy my breakfast and, I'm ashamed to say, sat and ate a **whole** bar of white chocolate.

I had a long discussion with the young German volunteer back at the Monastery: he was a student on an environmental course at … York University.

I told him that my sister and her husband lived near there: it worried him a bit, probably in case I was going to follow up by asking his name and address and visit him. So I didn't upset him further.

I found a very nice restaurant round the corner, serving a great Pilgrim Meal.

The lady in charge even smiled as she shoved solitary pilgrims together to share tables and save space. I ended up with the delectable Charlotte, who was an aspiring actress and was hurrying back to Germany to play a lead role in a forthcoming film.

She pouted deliciously, and went through the entire range of her theatrical expressions for my benefit. I even bought her a drink: but I let her pay for her own meal.

Like me, she wolfed down a big plate of steak and chips like a good'un.

It was obviously from a muscular animal that must have put up a heck of a fight before ending up on Charlotte's plate.

We walked back to the Refuge together: well, at least part of the way, she nipped across the road into a bar full of young muscular pilgrims looking for a particular one with whom she'd previously walked for several days, and who she'd somehow carelessly lost.

Day 33

Samos to Barbadelo

14 km   121 km to go

Actually, it was a 19 km walk to Barbadelo, but it includes a big loop to get back on track from Samos. Just thought I'd mention it, in case you thought I was being a bit weedy.

I sat outside the Monastery on a bench to eat my breakfast, squeezing a yoghourt direct into my mouth as you do, wolfing down an orange and a banana, and making a delicious bocadillo from new cream cheese (I'd donated my several day old container to the starving street animals of Samos, who were clambering out of the waste bins even as I sat and ate), supermarket jam and the end of a brand new loaf of bread.

It was nice outside, before the heat of the day: good job it wasn't raining, because there were no seats or tables inside the Refuge, you just had to squat on your bed otherwise.

The first couple of kilometres were along uncluttered roads, before I turned up right towards Pascais.

I'd been making up ground steadily for the past kilometre on an old man in a blue three piece suit (suit, not suite!), a tie and a straw hat. He was unaware of this, or he might have put on a bit of a gallop; I took him at the turning with an 'Hola!' and 'Camino?', cocking my head towards the steep hill on the right.

He gestured to the main road: he indicated that I must be mad to reject a perfectly good flat road that would have taken me all the way to Sarria without necessarily breaking sweat.

It was a long kilometre climb up a well surfaced asphalt road. I guess it must have been laid in winter: had it been surfaced in mid-summer, it was so steep that the asphalt would have melted and run all the way down to the bottom and ended up in a huge black heap.

I turned downhill past the 12th century church of Santa Eulalia de Pascais: the guide book noted that 'the church porch is a good place for a rest/shelter', but I was too knackered to climb the steps to find out.

It took two kilometres to go downhill and cross the road and the Rio Oríbio which I'd left an hour or so earlier.

Now, another Pilgrim Law: whenever you stop for a pee, pilgrims appear, and you have to pretend either to be admiring the view or to be consulting your guide book.

More difficult for ladies, of course: at first, I had innocently thought that they'd merely lost their way when I saw them descending from bramble clad banks or woodland.

The last 5 km to Sarria was along a virtually unused country lane. I only saw one car for the entire hour and a half… and that was at the bar that didn't sell Kit Kat: but his *servicios*, tiled from floor to ceiling and the entire floor, contained a bath (and shower), a bidet, a washbasin, a toilet – but no paper!

I had a café con leche grande whilst I got over the shock: I stocked up with napkins from the dispenser on the table instead, and fortified myself with a high calory iced cake.

Should I stop at Sarria? I sat beside the sculpture in the main square with the Annoyed French Lady from the vaulted dormitory at Samos, and her henpecked husband Jean.

They were going home from here, to start again next year: but they were going to stay at the Refuge tonight.

The clouds had cleared and it was now baking hot. The town was conveniently situated at the top of the hill: if it had been invaded in the Middle Ages, the enemy, weighed down with armour, would probably be too tired to fight once they'd got to the top of the 5,000 steps (actually, there's only 48, but it feels like 5,000 with a heavy rucksack on your back) and would probably have settled for a nice cup of coffee and a bun.

We all made it to the Refuge, nestling on a corner: predominantly lady pilgrims were grouped picturesquely around it on the steps, looking like a school photograph on an outing.

It wasn't open for a couple of hours, so I carried on through the town, past the weekly market and the prison, which seemed empty. The rusting ornate bars across the windows didn't seem strong enough to restrain determined inmates: perhaps they knew when they were well off.

Once I'd crested the hill, I went down very steeply to the level from which I'd just started.

I spent a pleasant half an hour or so walking beside the main Madrid-La Coruña railway line before I joined a quiet 'green lane' and into steep oak woodland. I was photographing a ford over a little woodland stream from every conceivable angle and distance, when the delectable Charlotte sauntered past with a languid Film Première wave.

The cemetery at Barbadelo

She'd obviously failed to find her pilgrim soulmate in the bar last night.

The 2 km woodland hill took me through deserted villages, across a stream and past an impressive mansion which was being renovated by an army of workmen, through Barbadelo and up the hill to the lovely little Romanesque (whatever that means!) church, which had an impressive range of chests of drawers for the dead, and the Refuge.

Think what I'd saved myself tomorrow, if I'd stopped at Sarria!

A group of smiling pilgrims were seated on the sunbaked steps of the Refuge, secure in the knowledge that they were in the 22 man team. Their rucksacks, standing like tombstones against the wall and up the steps, seemed to stretch for ever. I added mine at the end and counted slowly.

I was number 18: I'd (theoretically) made it.

Two more arrived: they knew people further up the queue.

Veronica turned up in a taxi, to general merriment, and took her place amongst her friends Juan, Julia and Hermione up front.

I sat and chatted with Marco, from Brazil.

This was his first visit to Europe, although he'd been to Japan (doesn't count, Marco!)

He'd dreamed about doing the Camino for fifteen years, ever since he was eighteen.

'So you're, um, 33, Marco?' He looked amazed: 'How do you know?'

'Oh, I sort of just guessed', I said. He shook his head in bewilderment and told his friends.

They inspected me with similar amazement.

Marco had started at León, and now he was set for Santiago.

He'd come to find The Truth.

'What is The Truth?' he asked.

I shook my head: 'I don't know, Marco'.

I made it onto the team: number 21.

But when I got upstairs, I found that a (as opposed to 'the') girl friend of one of the team had been allotted a space from way behind me: and an injured pilgrim was already occupying a prime central bunk.

So I was off the team, consigned to a sleeping mat in the day room!

I appealed. The lady Hospitalero roared up the stairs: there was a brisk battle in Spanish. She removed the injured pilgrim, who was there because she hadn't been able to walk for a day, to the day room, and gave me a lower bunk in view of my age.

The original occupant had to clamber up above, but he didn't seem to mind too much.

As I lay on my bunk, I had a fantastic view through the

window of the Galician hills over which I'd just walked, and beyond which lay Sarria in the distance.

Fortunately, Charlotte had gone on to Ferreiros, eager to make up ground to get back for her imminent demanding first major role in a feature film. If she hadn't pressed on, I wouldn't have made the team, even with the back-up of the Hospitalero: and I didn't fancy sacrificing my bunk for a mattress, even for Charlotte!

There was a spotless kitchen next door to the washrooms and toilets. No wonder it was spotless, though: it had never been used! No pots, pans, cutlery: the cupboards wouldn't open, and the stove had never been connected!

But I was glad to see a First Aid box prominently displayed on the wall: it obviously had high priority, and we could all rest assured in an emergency with a bottle of Retidine, some Sun Block 50, a jar of fruit salts and an almost empty tube of antibiotic ointment to cover all medical eventualities.

There was a caravan snack-bar in a sheltered orchard up the hill behind the Refuge: and, 150 metres further (if you could make it) a distinctly more upmarket Restaurant, the Casa de Carmen, next to the village pump.

Carmen (if she's still there) also lets rooms. I knew instantly that it was upmarket (which means expensive) because it had a lobby, with comfortable seating and a stack of glossy publications which even included a Spanish house plant magazine!

There's posh for you, as they say in Wales!

It obviously catered for the Establishment rather than the rough end of the market: they reinforced this by not opening the restaurant until 8.30 pm. Pilgrims, of course, are supposed to be getting ready to settle down for the night at this time: or, in the

The refuge at Barbadelo behind the grandstand

case of Barbadelo, not.

I strolled back to the Refuge: my washing was drying nicely on long strings stretched between trees on the village Brown (as opposed to Green) in front of the long, white concrete spectator stand in which a family of cyclists had camped for the night.

What could spectators be spectating from there, I wondered: my Spanish wasn't up to finding out.

The Village Brown is flat and level, but only about 60 metres square: and now, it's got a dozen steadily maturing trees growing around and even **on** the fringes. And it's got an unvandalised phone box in the near corner: they don't seem to go in for that sort of thing in rural Galicia.

True, someone has emptied a barbecue in another corner, and a cow has been doing 'things' on it in a random pattern, whilst someone else has been distributing bottle tops, laced with broken glass, across the centre: but it's still an obvious asset for the village.

Any suggestions for it's use on a £20 note, please.

I was sitting on a shady bench outside the Refuge, watching pilgrim life unfold.

A young lady was cradling the head of her companion in her lap, stroking his hair with a far away look in her eyes.

An enormous lady, who looked as if she'd got a chest of drawers up her jumper, came and sat beside her equally well endowed husband.

He's just pushed me up the bench to get more room to expand, and got out his diary.

Perhaps he knows what I'm writing.

Lights from isolated houses and hamlets were dotting the distant hills.

Pilgrims on bicycles were still toiling past on their way to Portomarín, and taking five minutes out to get a self-service *sello* from the table outside the door.

Marco and his friend were engaged in trying to find The Truth beside the Caravan snack-bar. An impressive array of empty bottles of San Miguel stood mute testimony to their efforts. Nobody could say they hadn't tried.

But the truth is, Marco, the harder you work to find the answer, the more difficult it becomes.

They stayed debating the issue until well after 11 pm.

The door of the Refuge, fortunately, had been left open to let in air. Thank goodness it had, because the beautiful airy dormitory was soon restored to stifling heat when fat Juan and his travelling companions determinedly closed the windows and drew the curtains. My socks still lay outside on the window sill: I didn't like to get them in. I scrambled out of my sleeping bag to try to get a little cooler, just keeping my feet inside to guard against mosquitoes (apparently, recent research shows that they go for cheesy feet!)

My bunk had also turned out to be child's size.

The builders had obviously miscalculated and had to saw six inches off the end, to get it in.

I found out by accident when I flung myself full length and banged my head on the end: even when I stuck my feet through the bars onto the window ledge, I couldn't stretch and certainly couldn't turn over. So I was confined to a compressed foetal position, like the Hospitalero at Samos (except that he'd done it standing up, which was infinitely harder).

I resembled a very large foetus in a very small womb.

I checked next morning, after everybody else had gone: yes, **their** bunks would have accommodated me full length with ease. When they'd grabbed their bunks 'on the hoof' yesterday afternoon, they'd obviously known a thing or two!

The pilgrim who'd been forced to swap bunks with me, turned out not only to be very small (so he'd fitted the bunk nicely), but also to be Marco's particular friend: he stumbled in about 11.30 pm and within seconds was challenging Simian, the Worlds Greatest Snorer, for his title. I reached up, and shoved him hard in the back between the slats, and he stopped.

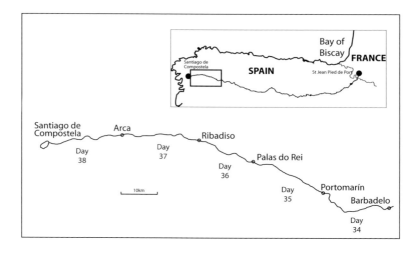

11

The Worst, the Best and Even Better!

Day 34

Barbadelo to Portomarín

17 km   107 km to go

I left the dormitory empty so that I could switch on the lights and settle down to a leisurely breakfast beside my bunk. Next door, only Marco snored on: his friend, from the bunk above me, had deserted him. I hoped Marco had found The Truth: it wouldn't be for want of trying, judging from his efforts last night outside the mobile snackbar, if he failed!

I couldn't find any space to eat in the dayroom, because it was full of sleeping cyclists: they get up late!

What did I eat? Oh, you know: the usual.

It was getting light later in the mornings now: it was still dark at 07.00, and I watched the dawn break as I strolled along (once I'd got over the sharp shock of the first 2 km uphill drag). The Camino led through almost deserted 'green lanes', stone walls bordering the sometimes stony, often sandy track.

I was fascinated by the small fields full of 'cabbages on sticks' beside many farmhouses. The bare stems were often ten

If you like cabbage, this is the place for you!

or twelve feet tall, picked bare of leaves apart from the crown that remained: as I passed, a lady popped out of her house and broke off a few of the top leaves and took them back inside as a main ingredient for nourishing Galician meat, cabbage and potato soup.

I came across the first *horreos,* which are so typical of Galicia and fascinated me enormously. I couldn't resist photographing them: all the way to Santiago!

Want to see a collection of *horreo* photographs? No, not 'horror', *'horreo'.*

What's that? What's a *horreo?* Oh, sorry: I forgot to mention it. It's a long, narrow rectangular stone, brick or even wooden storehouse, with a pitched roof, and raised several feet above the ground on stilts or piles. There is a cross at one end of the roof and a decorative knob at the other, and they were/are used to store potatoes, corncobs etc.

Probably kept the rats out.

They can be up to 20 metres long, but most are much shorter, perhaps a quarter of this length.

And whenever I saw them, I got a great thrill! They are so mystical, so unique to Galicia.

Long striding pilgrims began to pass with determined expressions, eyes fixed (metaphorically speaking) on Santiago:

A horreo

where they'd spent the night, I couldn't guess.

Perhaps at Casa Carmen: it had looked as if it was somewhere for the ultra fit to maintain their strength.

Gradually, the backmarkers began to pass and repass each other, stopping regularly to admire the distant views. There were lots of little bars in the first 9 km, contrary to what guide books would have you believe. I stopped at Ferreiros and, there was my lovely Elisabetha! She'd pulled a muscle days ago, but she was still walking, leg strapped up. She had her same tired brave smile and I know that she'll reach Santiago.

I was sad to see that she also had been afflicted by red hair.

There were also groups of youngsters preparing for the 'Jubilee', Holy Year next year: what these preparations involved, so far ahead, I couldn't even guess.

Whatever, they were very eager.

They were being marshalled by **another** Timothy Bull

Wash day in rural Galicia

lookalike; they probably have a central laboratory in Galicia where they are cloned, and very effective they are for instilling discipline into the young.

I might be able to outstare **one** singly as I had at Samos: but if there was more than one, say a small group of them, I'd probably bow and gesture to them obsequiously to go ahead.

A throng of cyclists sped past, barely a day from Santiago: and I suddenly realised that I was now less than 100 km away myself. 98, actually.

I loved the half kilometre marking posts: they might not be accurate to the metre, but you could judge your progress and I got a tingling feeling as they counted down to Portomarín.

Surely it must be just over this hill? And there it was, just as the guide book had suggested.

Now, Portomarín had once lain at the bottom of the river valley below: but it had been flooded in the 1960's when they had dammed the river Miño to make a reservoir and the new replacement town had been built on the hill above.

But the fortified Romanesque church of San Nicolás had been taken to pieces stone by stone and painstakingly rebuilt in the new town centre: you can still see the numbers on the stones.

It was half a kilometre across the long bridge over the reservoir: and yes, the town **was** now built on a hill. A **big** hill, in fact: and even when you reached the top, you were **still** only just over 1,200 ft up. So it was effectively a 'low' spot of the Camino: which meant there was a whole lot of 'up' to come!

Once you'd got to the top of the main road, and turned into Portomarín with it's colonnaded town centre packed with shady bars and shops sloping gently past the gloomy public park down towards the river below, with narrow, rambling streets leading off at either side, you would never have guessed that it hadn't been there for centuries.

The builders had achieved the seemingly impossible and achieved built-in dilapidation.

I left my rucksack in a strange line with several branch lines outside the small, low, whitewashed Refuge and sat in a bar opposite the church so that I could sip a can of cool Nestea and count the numbers on the stones. I got a *sello* **there**, as well.

I kept nipping back to check whether the Refuge had opened early: they usually do, they list an opening hour rather like a 'starter for five' just because they have to put down something specific rather than saying 'when the Hospitalero has finished his or her lunch and/or siesta and done the shopping'.

Lots of other pilgrims were sitting outside similar bars, doing the same thing, to rouse their colleagues with a rallying cry when the Hospitalero was spotted.

Sometimes, of course, Hospitaleros would sidle up incognito and insinuate themselves into the Refuge: but generally, they had 'the look' about them.

Although the Refuge is listed as having 160 places, most of them are in the gymnasium opposite: I only just made it into the 36 person team in the main Refuge in next to last place.

I got an upper bunk: bunks were so closely packed that you could virtually step from one to the other.

Even with one of the windows open, and the curtains drawn, the heat was stifling. The temperature felt like the *meseta* Refuges plus quite a lot, already: and this, remember, was before the pilgrims had sealed themselves in for the night. Unlike most Refuges, there was nowhere outside to sleep: for instance, on the Village Brown or in tents in the park.

So, 'If you can't stand the heat, stay out of the ... dormitory'.

Lots of the Barbadelo crew had made the team, including fat Juan: Julia, Hermione and Veronica (who'd made it by taxi yesterday as well) had all arrived by taxi, and seemed relatively fresh.

Veronica had walked the Camino before, though, so it didn't matter too much, she indicated: and she'd climbed Mount Kilimanjaro as well (though not all on the same day, of course, and certainly not by taxi).

Now, I do appreciate the Refuges: we couldn't do without them, and the Hospitaleros and Volunteers are marvellous. But ... if there was a grading system for Refuges, Portomarín would be bottom, and even lower if it were possible.

The toilets not only had no toilet paper, there wasn't even a toilet paper holder: there weren't even marks on the wall where one had been ripped off.

There were no locks on the doors (I speak only for the men, you understand: surprisingly, the sexes were segregated here!): one door didn't even close.

You need a plug for basins throughout, anyway, so that didn't count.

But there were dire penalties for washing your clothes in the kitchen (don't know what they were, but they were dire): you had to walk a couple of hundred yards up the hill to the municipal wash place, situated outside a large block of flats on an uneven litter strewn area of ground.

There were four vast deep sinks, each a metre or more square, into each of which the usual ridged concrete scrubbing board sloped.

Each was served by it's own tap: two of them worked. Water, surprisingly, was initially scalding hot: I almost dropped what I was washing from sheer pain. Good job I didn't, though: my sink was one of the two with a tap, but it was also the one with three inches of evil smelling stagnant water in the bottom, thick with greasy soap powder, leaves and insects that had been overcome by the fumes before they had managed to struggle free. The odd garment stuck out above the water: nobody had bothered to retrieve it. The drainage hole, even if you could identify where it might be (probably at the back), would need either an exceptionally brave man or a raving lunatic to unblock it.

After the first blast of hot water, though, it settled down to cold and normal.

I kept a very tight grip on what I was washing: if it had fallen, I would have left it to rot amidst the stench.

Then I carried my washing back to the Refuge and hung it on the line in the back yard.

As for the kitchens: well, the further west you walk, the more basic or even non-existent they become. As I said before, it's a poorer area: and this makes sure that pilgrim business is transferred to the bars and shops around. I can understand this: that's fine. They did a roaring trade throughout the summer.

But the kitchen at Portomarín lures you in, then bashes you firmly on the head.

It was quite large, with a nice kitchen table that proved, even on cursory inspection, to be so dirty that you had to spread newspaper or polythene bags on top before you ate. The shelves all around the walls were covered with dead flies, probably (like the pilgrims) overcome by the heat. There were no utensils, anyway, so it didn't really matter.

The stove was filthy: the rings were rusting. I don't think that it was usable, anyway.

I ate my breakfast in there next day: I was the only one, and took care that nothing touched the table top. Then I threw away the newspaper that had covered it.

So, if you've got to stay at Portomarín, just use it for sleeping: and if you've got any other option, take it!

Oh yes, I forgot to mention probably the only 'plus' (apart from having security and a roof over your head): pilgrims got **free admission** to the municipal swimming pool down the road – but they had to pay €1 for the compulsory cap. Perhaps the attendant knew what Refuge pillows were like.

But the café/bars were great.

Veronica acted as 'broker' with introductions to Juan, Julia and Hermione: I pretended that I hadn't been aware that we might not have hit it off at Barbadelo.

Why was that? Oh, I might tell you later: on the other band, I might not …

We got on very well: Camino friends for ever.

I was extolling the wonderful views from the Alto do Poya. Juan and his ladies smiled. Veronica coughed: 'Excuse me, Harry', she said: 'It is **Poyo,** not **Poya**. Poya is – er, not nice'.

'What does it mean?'

'Ah', she said: 'in Spanish, it means 'dick'.

I ate a nourishing bacon, eggs and chips and went back to the Refuge.

Day 35

Portomarín to Palas do Rei

24 km   90 km to go

I'd never worried about not being able to complete the Camino before, even way back at St Jean. I'd had no doubt about succeeding. But at Portomarín, I suddenly began to think 'What if I drop out **now**? What if I break a leg, or pull a muscle? Or get food poisoning? What will people think if I get back without succeeding?'

'Oh, bad luck!' to my face: whilst behind my back (I prefer it that way, it doesn't upset me) it would be 'Oh, yeah, couldn't quite make it: broken leg/food poisoning, you know' and smile knowingly.

And of course, to me I would have just… failed.

I began to take more care of myself!

The 'new me' made a mistake at once: I slept in until 07.00!

It was to be a long day, as well.

I had to retrace my steps down to a bridge across the river, then leant into a long gradually steepening hill above the river through shady woods.

Galicia usually consists of long gradual **uphills** followed by equally long **downhills** through the 'green lanes'. Today, there were long uphills followed by short downhills; 7 km up, 1 km down, before I reached the café/bar at Gonzar! It could only get easier from here, I reckoned.

Elisabetha was there: her leg was still painful, and she was going to overnight there.

So we had a final photograph and a (chaste) kiss: then I was off towards Palas do Rei.

She looked very vulnerable, and I hope she'll find somebody to look after her.

Suddenly, I began to be aware that I might not get into the 'team' at Palas do Rei: I was sitting outside the Refuge at Eirexe beside the road, and I was passed by fourteen pilgrims! They looked a bit beat-up, true: I sprang (slowly) from my seat and resolved to 'take them all'! I pulled back most of them over the next few kilometres: but then a trio of young girls pulled away, and half a dozen more tough looking middle-aged pilgrims strode past.

I crossed the main road over a bridge, and was caught by a couple of cyclists from Los Angeles, with most of their worldly possessions piled on and around their bikes.

'We've got a son in Los Angeles: in Yorba Linda', I said, trying to 'bond'.

'Wow! That's near us!' said Jack: 'About a hundred miles down the road'.

They had altimeters on their bikes: we were 610 m up, said Jeannie.

She said most of the climb was over: only two little pimples over the next 12 km.

I warmed to her immediately: turned out she lied! And she'd seemed such a nice girl!

There was an almost immediate mammoth long slow 3 km uphill, plus lots of sharp ups and downs (pimples!) before the steady 2 km down to Palas do Rei.

I passed the sparkling new information centre beside the track: it sported the slogan *Peregrinos aseos* (sit down toilets for pilgrims) in huge letters over the door.

I should have asked for further information, but I didn't have time, with the Pilgrim Pack closing: I contented myself with asking the young lady in the crisp white blouse behind the desk if **this** was the Albergue de Peregrinos.

'No, one kilometre down the track', she said brightly, a finger to her lips (don't know why, perhaps she was blowing me a kiss, or there was somebody asleep inside).

I set off downhill like a scalded cat, looking over my shoulder constantly in case a mob of chasing pilgrims was in hot pursuit.

Through the streets of Palas do Rei, and down a flight of steps to the Refuge. It was as good there as Portomarín was bad!

I was welcomed in perfect English by a young lady university student, who told me that she was shortly to go to France to teach French. Why? I persevered, but got nowhere. Ah well, not to worry.

It was 1.30 pm: my efforts had been in vain. I would have to sleep on my sleeping mat in the enormous day room: or in the entrance hall. No mattresses. That's fine, I said: no worries.

'But' said the young lady, as if having a second thought: 'We do have a room here for old people, over 65: but we did not like to mention it to you in case you did not want to accept Charity. Would this interest you?'

'**Me**? **Would** it? Yes, **please**!' I said: '**I'll** accept Charity!'.

After all, I'd spent sixty six years working to get Charity like this: now appeared to be the time to cash in on my efforts.

She showed me up to the OAP's room, and unlocked the door. Two two tier bunks, with pillows, and lots of space around: and through a door was an ensuite toilet (with paper!), washbasin, shower – and bath! There was even a towel beside the washbasin, and the floor was dry! And a lock on the door!

I was the first OAP in residence!

Was I happy, or what!

I sat in the bath (first bath for years, but I thought I'd better make maximum use of the facilities), and washed my hair. No shower curtain, but I didn't get a drop on the floor: usual practise, naughty bits outwards, face shower head inwards.

I even shaved: Ada's razor was sure earning it's keep.

The next OAP arrived: a pugnacious lady, with the look of an unsuccessful boxer, and the leader of a party with which I'd been jousting over the past few kilometres.

Then it all fell apart.

She left the door open.

Next thing, a young lady with raven hair had locked herself into the washroom.

An hour or so later, she came out: the floor was swamped, and the washbasin clogged with black hair. There was so much that I wondered if it had been loose: there was enough to make up a modest sized pan scourer.

A grizzled 68 year old from Slovenia grabbed the third bunk: then a young lady in her mid twenties grabbed the fourth bunk (don't know how **she** got in!) and with her partner from the lobby dominated the washroom for much of the rest of the afternoon.

Two young Swedes, Charlotte looking as coquettish and pouty as ever, Juan and his gang, and Veronica had also arrived, as well as half the others from Barbadelo and Portomarín. It was getting like an Old School Reunion. There was a bad outbreak of red hair there, as well: with one lady, it had developed into a flaming luminous orange display. I hoped it wasn't catching, and wondered whether I should keep my hat on.

Itzia had the most open dazzling smile that I had ever seen. She was lovely. She was standing in the lobby, whilst I was waiting for a Japanese girl to stop monopolising the French Teacher behind the desk so that I could ask her something deep and meaningful (like, 'Where's the nearest good restaurant, and what local dish should I try before I return home and get back to egg, sausage and chips?')

Itzia worked as a translator (so she spoke perfect English).

'We live in Cork, in Ireland, now' she said.

'So you love an Irishman now, as well as living there?'

'No' she said: 'I **live** with him, but I don't **love** him'.

But she was still walking the Camino for him (Carlos: he was Spanish, and she'd taken him with her. It wasn't a normal Irish name, I'd worked out).

They'd walked the Camino successfully together last year: but since they got home, he'd started drinking heavily. He'd stopped now: but she was walking the Camino to make sure that he **stayed** stopped.

Itzia was very spiritual, a vegan for the past year, and an opportunist for ever. Midway through the Camino this year, she'd had the opportunity to fly to Norway, via London, to do the pilgrimage to the Shrine of St Olaf. After she'd finished, she'd rejoined the Camino and worked for a week as a volunteer at Estella with a Canadian girl, who'd decided to give up the Camino.

One night, they'd 'escaped' from the Refuge and got picked up by a lorry driver who, like everybody else I guess, fell for Itzia.

'I am going to drive you both to Santiago to embrace (the statue of) St James, then take you (the Canadian girl) to Madrid, and return you (Itzia) to the exact spot where I picked you up'.

This he did that night: next day, Itzia said, she walked only one kilometre, she was so tired.

She'd walked with a young man for several days, she said, who swore non-stop and spat at the Camino.

'Why do you use such language? Why do you hate the Camino?' she said, after several days (she must either have been extremely forbearing, or not particularly inquisitive).

His brother had been the sportsman in the family, he said: he had been paralysed in an accident, and he was doing this for him to show that he was his legs from now onwards.

Remarkable things seemed to happen around Itzia.

We went to a bar for a coffee together but, as a Vegan, she didn't fancy eggs, sausage and chips.

As I came back to the Refuge, she was wrapped up in her sleeping bag on a bench in the lobby. I went up to the OAP's room: the washroom was now empty at last.

Day 36

Palas do Rei to Ribadiso

26 km   66 km to go

I was even more frightened today of not completing the Camino than I had been yesterday.

The Old People's Dormitory emptied early. The muscular lady who looked like an Unsuccessful Boxer was away by 04.45: no reservations about not waking other old people for **her**!

The Slovenian gentleman was intent on doing 33 km today, and reaching Santiago the day after: he also left well before 06.00.

I left the Young Lady Who Had Monopolised The Bathroom For Much Of The Previous Afternoon With Her Boyfriend still sleeping soundly: I guess that the experience had tired her.

I ate in the deserted kitchen and checked the washing lines: it was a claustrophobic little area in which a mass of garments hung together damply in a shaded courtyard, but it worked. No, nothing left on the line. I breathed a sigh of relief.

Refuges came thick and fast from here to Santiago, to cater for pilgrims intent on walking the minimum distance to get their Compostela, 100 km.

I even passed two 'unofficial' ones before I arrived at Casanova, which itself was only 6 km from Palas do Rei.

No, 'Casanova' doesn't signify 'naughties' as you might think if you read the saucy books of the fifties or watched the recent television documentary about the imaginative gentleman who shared the name.

It just means 'new house': and in the case of the Refuge there, it simply wasn't true.

There was a drinks stall nearby: I stocked up on carbohydrates with a can of sugary drink.

It was typical Galicia: the long steep 3 km ups, and the long 3 km downs along the 'green lanes'. We scarcely touched a road: and the dusty tracks were now winding through shady eucalyptus groves, with their pungent perfume.

I shouldn't think that many pilgrims reached Santiago with chest infections after **that**!

There was yet another Refuge after a further couple of miles, at Leboreiro.

It was billed as 'Basic, no beds or mattresses: water problems in summer'.

I resisted the temptation and slumped into a bar for my usual. It was packed with pilgrims.

I pushed on through Melide, 5.5 km further, where there is a huge Refuge: was I glad later that I had, I'd have been beating myself up for days if I'd weakened and stayed there!

I'd been tempted to drop in at a *Pulperia* to try the local delicacy of 'spiced octopus in wine on wooden platters with bread and white Ribeiro wine'. '*Pulperia*', though, rather put me off: it suggested something soft and repulsive. Even so, it had been on my mind for days to try, but it turned out that, following the Prestige oil spill disaster off the coast, there was a severe shortage of octopus (or octopi?).

Probably all for the best: I'm a spaghetti, eggs and chips man myself, I guess.

The Camino was beginning to level out now: we'd dropped a couple of thousand foot from Alto de Poyo (spelling!) and now there were lots of little energy sapping ups and downs, mainly through shady woodland, from here to Santiago across the river valleys.

The last couple of the 26 km to Ribadiso were down a steep hill: I reluctantly passed a bar off the road to the right but it didn't matter, because I went back up there later.

The Refuge was just the other side of the little river bridge.

I soon found that, if Portomarín was below the bottom of the list, then Ribadiso was above the top (if you follow what I mean!)

It was incredible: I could be a volunteer there for ever. Only problem, I can't speak Spanish beyond the 100 word pilgrim vocabulary, and that's not really enough when lots of people are asking all sorts of extraordinary questions in Spanish at the same time.

It's staffed by volunteers, replaced on a weekly or fortnightly basis. The only qualifications seem to be that a) you've completed the Camino yourself and b) you speak reasonably fluent Spanish. Oh yes, and I guess that you like **people**!

All this seemed pretty reasonable.

The Refuge had been a former pilgrim hospital, restored and able to welcome 62 pilgrims in bunks plus an unlimited number on mats, and a vast area of grass beyond the Refuge and beside the treelined river (but out of mosquito range!) for camping.

The OAP lady who looked like an Unsucessful Boxer was already there (well, so she should be, after all I'd given her two hours start!)

So was fat Juan: so were his lady companions (one of whom turned out to be his wife, but I never found out which one although I kept a sharp eye on them all for almost a week) Julia and Hermione. They'd arrived by taxi, as one (or both) of them was having trouble with their feet. The delectable Charlotte also arrived by taxi, still suffering from her stomach (the bit peeping out from beneath her crop top looked alright to me, though!): she took to her bunk hoping to walk tomorrow.

Gobby, a teacher from Cork, was there: she'd started from Palas do Rei that morning after me, had stopped to look at the churches along the way, and still got to Ribadiso an hour **before** me!

The two young Swedes had copped out, and stopped at Melide.

There was – **WOW!** I'd just seen the lady with orange luminous hair! Coming out of a dark room, it's enough to unsettle a pilgrim for hours!

There were just lots of faces that I recognised with an 'Hola!' or 'Que tal?' or 'OK?', and long discussions in pidgin Spanish/English/French, a sort of contemporary Esperanto, about the day's walk, where we were going to stop the next day and where we were going to eat!

I arrived at 1.30: Juan told me that they'd been registering for half an hour, in 'room full batches of eight or ten'. There were two Hospitaleros on duty: even so, it took 75 minutes for the

Ribadiso. My bunk is bottom left; Juan's now is top left!

Chief Hospitalero to process us!

He gave an entirely new meaning to the words 'painstaking' and 'slow'.

His Sidekick then ushered us to our room.

Myself, Juan and his friends scraped into the last room: after that, it would have been sleeping mats.

I don't think they had an OAP room there. I was allocated a top bunk: after watching my inept attempts to get on board (Deliberate? Moi?), Juan nobly agreed to swap. It just showed how we had bonded since Barbadelo! Now, he was almost like a father to me!

Shifting his enormous bulk onto a top bunk must have involved considerable effort: but I didn't like him to think that I didn't appreciate his generosity, so I let him get on with it.

The small dormitories, furnished with polished wooden bunks with firm steps and with a locker beside each (no rucksacks on the floor, the Sidekick warned sternly), were nice and airy.

There were big, very clean separate toilet blocks (with paper!) for men and women about fifty metres away, and similarly segregated showers with warm water **where you could regulate the heat**: lots of deep sinks: long clothes lines **in the sun** (some Refuges, like Palas do Rei, tuck them away in the shade).

I came across a coyly worded reference to the effect that, with the toilets 50 metres away, there was a 'night facility'. I never did find out what or where it was.

The kitchen was massive: and if you just felt like relaxing, after you'd done the washing (mine was dry and crinkly as usual, in three hours!), you could sit on long shady benches or on the stone steps beside the river and dangle your feet in the cold water.

What words did my vocabulary search come up with to describe Ribadiso?

Only one, **idyllic**.

But Ribadiso is a long way from support: so, bring your own food or toil back up the steep sunbaked hill to the bar, which has a delicate pale blue horreo outside: hope it's not functional, with eggs and chips stored up there!

I trekked back to the bar about 7.00pm when, theoretically, the heat of the day was over.

It wasn't.

Sweat poured off me when I arrived and fed the drinks machine outside with euros. It was baking hot **inside** the bar, as well: I held a cold Nestea to my forehead as I bought my bananas, bread and yoghourt for breakfast and inspected the Pilgrim Menu, and even that only gave temporary relief.

The menu was, well, limited.

Spaghetti alone, without dressing: but they provided a cardboard carton of tomato sauce so that you could mix it to your taste.

Lamb and chips: or alternatively, chips and lamb. As I don't like (can't **stand**) lamb, this posed a problem.

So they made an exception for me: I dined on two fried eggs, swimming in a sea of oil, and chips.

Santiago Tart followed: they call it **Bakewell** Tart in Derbyshire, where I come from. Gobby was at the next table, with three **more** teachers from Cork.

It was like a Cork Education Authorities Outing.

I joined them for a chat: one of the two other lady teachers took a very dim view of my having left half a bottle of wine on my table, which had been hurriedly removed by the waitress and poured back into the tanker outside the back door, as she'd been eager to boost her alcohol intake for the day and some space still remained.

They were on a 'fact finding visit', intent on bringing a party of up to ten students the following May or June to walk part of the Camino.

Today was their first day: they'd started from Palas do Rei at 08.10, they'd walked 26 km in the heat of the day and arrived at 16.30, and they'd had to sleep on mats!

So it hadn't been an ideal start.

Next year was Holy Year, as I pointed out: if they arrived at 16.30 **then**, they'd be lucky to get space for a sleeping mat even out on the road!

I don't even think that they had a Guide Book with them.

I'm glad I wouldn't be one of their students.

Day 37

Ribadiso to Arca

23 km   40 km to go

If you like starting the day with a steep 2.5 km climb, then this is the day for you!

Juan clambered down from the top bunk early: his fat hairy legs were waving about desperately, looking for some sort of foothold (either he'd ignored the steps, or didn't trust their weight bearing capabilities) just after 4.30.

I pretended I was still asleep.

Veronica told me afterwards that he was planning to walk the entire remaining 40 km to Santiago that day, with Julia and Hermione following by taxi a little later.

The delectable Charlotte did the same: her stomach, it seemed, was still not right.

I'd wanted to set off at 06.00, the hour before which no Refuge is supposed to open it's door. Actually, most pilgrims have escaped well before then.

But I couldn't force open the door into the kitchen, where I'd stored my breakfast, until one of the mass of pilgrims sleeping inside on their sleeping mats and blocking the door got up and unlocked it. She was rather annoyed to be disturbed.

So I breakfasted (banana, dry bread, yoghourt, jam, cream cheese and a bottle of water, but not necessarily in that order) standing in the courtyard behind the main gate, waiting for the first shafts of sunlight to show in the morning sky above Arzúa.

Arzúa is a long, functional town: it has everything.

It was also at the top of the first of the three big climbs in the first 8 km. After that, there was nothing significant: it was pure

Last café con leche on the Camino. It's a long way to carry a guitar

magic, sandy tracks through predominantly eucalyptus woods and scarcely crossing a road.

I dropped into the bar at Calzada for the 'usual': and a slice of thin dried *empanada*. It looked as if it had been intended for a much smaller baking tray than the one it finally occupied, and rolled out to fit. The lady behind the bar let me choose my own slice: I went for one in the middle rather than the crusty bits round the side, which looked pretty short of filling.

Thomas from Germany, and his wife and friend, were sitting under the shady grape vine with a group that were (so they told me) a gentleman from the *Times* with his wife and family, who was writing up the story for his paper. Me, I'm more a *Daily Mail* sort of chap myself.

The bar looked like a 'summer bar', hurriedly cobbled together around a dusty yard full of flimsy plastic San Miguel chairs and tables: but it really fulfilled a need! I got another 'fix' at a bar above the road near Salceda, with a toilet into which I wouldn't have backed a self respecting horse.

I'm sure it wasn't like that all the time, though: perhaps the cleaner was shifting anxiously from foot to foot outside, waiting for me to come out, so that she could rush in and purify it before the evening rush.

Halfway up the hill beside the road, I overtook a young Spanish lady, her head festooned with lank dreadlocks that hung down to her shoulders. She looked like Medusa.

She was limping painfully, and badly dehydrated. I gave her one of my bottles of water, and we walked to the bar at the top of the hill.

Her family soon arrived, to my relief. They largely ignored her, and ploughed ahead.

I bought her a drink, and did the same: but only **after** I was certain that she was alright to continue. After all, what are friends for: and there's not much chance of Search and Rescue in the middle of the Camino if it all goes wrong.

I almost caught up with a couple of sturdy pilgrims carrying what looked like a double bass (might have been a big guitar, I suppose) between them, holding straps on each side: but they looked over their shoulders and saw me closing them down, and soon pulled away.

The track turned off the main road, past the memorial to Guillermo Watt, a 69 year old pilgrim who'd died at that spot on August 25th 1993, just a day from Santiago! Tenth anniversary tomorrow! There were flowers beside the memorial.

A few kilometres further, I passed the isolated Refuge at Santa Irene.

The Teachers From Cork On A Fact Finding Visit, and the New English Roses from Barbadelo, where she'd been sitting dreamily stroking his hair, were already outside, cooking in the sun and waiting for sanctuary. I'd met the New English Roses at Palas do Rei also: there, they'd been walking up the stairs so they'd obviously arrived early enough to get a bunk.

Turned out she was from Chicago, and he from Birmingham: you'd never have guessed, just by looking at them!

It was downhill through the woods after this sunbaked crest: I was as usual just at the back of the first flush of pilgrims.

I reached the main road. The Camino was signposted into the cool woods across the road: the Refuge, a sign at my elbow suggested, was a mere 200 metres up the main road to my left. Really, there was no choice! Even though it was a Spanish 200m, after a kilometre or so on the hard shoulder I was obviously getting close.

The big stone Refuge was just off the road, behind the Post Office: it looked over the tree filled valley at the back.

Room for 120 on three floors. Most of the pilgrims from Ribadiso had made the team, patiently waiting to register. I tucked in behind Thomas, who'd just qualified as a part-time lawyer at the University of Cape Town, and his wife and friend.

Veronica missed the cut for the fifth successive time: another sleeping mat on the floor!

Might have something to do with her habit of stopping for lunch on the way. She certainly disapproved of the fact that there had been a special room for OAPs at Palas do Rei.

I think that there was a similar room for the elderly at Arca: whilst I was queueing, I poked my head round the door of an empty room with two nice single **beds**, but decided to keep it to myself in case of an emergency (like, being consigned to a sleeping mat in the day room).

But it turned out alright, after all, so I didn't need to alienate Veronica: I got the bottom bunk, right beside the washroom door, next to last place.

I sat on the narrow patio in front of the Refuge, watching pilgrims on foot or bicycle labouring up the road for the final 17 kilometres to Santiago, pursued by heavy lorries.

I chatted with Carol, who had also started from St Jean, with her boyfriend (who'd gone back, hope they meet up again!), son and friend. The latter two had stuck by her, I'm glad to say.

She was an ex-PA, and a former Fitness Instructor on Cruise Ships (probably not both at the same time, though): now she was a mature Law Student at Newcastle University.

Her next project was walking St Anne's Way.

But she soon drifted away: she was engrossed in a new form of Patience (the card game, not the sort that courting couples used to play in the old days, waiting for her parents to go to bed), and didn't want to waste a minute.

The kitchen was enormous and immaculate, stocked with every imaginable cooking utensil, the shelves full of upmarket leftovers (rice and pasta some of which even had several days remaining before their sell-by date was reached, for instance) and looked like something from an advertisement in Country Life.

There were washing and drying machines in there, as well: and a fantastic view out of the window.

This was the first Refuge kitchen in the middle of a Galician town that I found to be functional: and it was a great meeting place.

Most in Galicia were designed to drive pilgrims to support local shops and bars.

Didn't bother me, though: I can't really cook anyway, and after heating up soup, I tend to get lost.

And I'm all for supporting local café/bar/restaurants: you can't go wrong with a three course meal, including wine and bread, for between €6 and €8 (£4 to £5.50).

Go on, spoil yourself, especially if you're by yourself: although I grant you, it's different if you're in a group.

There was an enormous sitting room, but it was now submerged beneath a sea of mattresses and sleeping mats. It wouldn't be long before the Refuge reached it's absolute maximum of 220, I guessed: there was now only the entrance hall to go!

Now, what about the washrooms?

Well, the showers were quite innovative.

There were neither doors nor shower curtains: just a waist high wall (tiled) round which you walked to reach the water bit.

It had the advantage that you could see instantly if a shower cubicle was occupied and, very often, the precise sex of the occupant. This seemed to bother nobody.

Cold water? Not quite, but it's warm weather, so what?

There were three toilets in our little block.

One had a plaque on the door, of a laid back gigolo in evening dress, which I guessed was intended for men: one had a plaque of a flamenco dancer sweeping across the floor (and getting the hem of her dress very dirty in the process, I guess!): and the third carried no plaque and was presumably intended for those who haven't yet made up their minds whether they are boys or girls.

There were half a dozen washbasins as well, providing good quality cold water for washing self and clothes (and lots of intricate washing lines on the dusty slope in front of the Refuge): in deference to my imminent arrival in Santiago, I gave my face a good going over with Ada's razor, which still came up to scratch (no, wrong word: it still worked, anyway).

Early start tomorrow?

Perhaps: must try to get my breakfast in. But it was Sunday, and Spain: I guessed that I'd have to get by on what I could find in the bottom of my rucksack, wrapped up in my numerous Sainsbury's carrier bags which had lasted for six weeks, and still worked!

I'd just had a fascinating conversation with a Brazilian from the **upper** bunk (important, as you'll realise later!) opposite mine.

He sat down beside me on my bunk: and after we'd agreed that Brazilians spoke Portuguese (something that he apparently already knew), he said cheerily 'United States of America' and paused, waiting for the full effect to sink in.

Then, 'England'. He didn't suggest any correlation between the two, and sat waiting in anticipation for my reply.

'The World', I replied: 'We are all people of the world', which seemed a suitably deep sort of statement.

He stared blankly, with an uncomprehending smile.

'North America' he countered: then, 'England'.

The conversation didn't appear to be getting any more stimulating: so after exchanging a few more smiles, I made my excuses (like 'bar') and left.

He still smiled cheerily, glad of this opportunity for conversation.

Such opportunities along the Camino must have been few.

The young lady on the bunk below his was welcoming a boy friend; it was, after all, almost 6 pm and they were both refreshed from a long siesta.

She was still welcoming him when I left for the Restaurant at 7, and when I returned at 9 (although by then it was almost dark, and I doubt that they could see what they were doing) – and even after lights out at 11.

The heat generated on this lower bunk, especially after the usual, almost mandatory, closing of all the windows before bed time to ensure maximum heat build-up, must have been intense: probably enough to warm a small town in winter, let alone the odd isolated house.

At one point he got up to go: but after a few chaste kisses, they fell back on to the bunk, presumably exhausted. I felt sad that he apparently lacked the energy to move back to his own dormitory.

I didn't like to look too closely: I fell asleep.

By the time I woke, still worried in case I cracked up before Santiago, he had gone.

There was a bar/restaurant up the road: but it had closed for the evening, possibly fearing intensive pilgrim pressure on a Sunday. I'd met Carol along the way: she decided to try to find a bar further up the hill. I went back to the one that I'd passed earlier in the day, when I was making my final thrust towards the Refuge. I hadn't stopped to inspect it then, because of pilgrim pressure for bunks: but it was filed away in the deep recesses of my keen, analytical mind.

The restaurant at the back was packed out with pilgrims: in the bar, the locals were engrossed in a karaoke contest. It was just like home.

At first I sat alone: but Thomas and his gang, and a few Austrian pilgrims, beckoned me over to fill the final place at their table.

Thomas told me that his surname was the same as a famous make of German beer ('but I am not of that family'). No, it wasn't Holsten Pils.

He wanted to buy an English Bible for the **other** Thomas: hope I'm not confusing you, I mean the Irish pilgrim with the long white hair and beard who we'd met at Ribadiso and who spends the winters at Fatima and the summers slowly walking the Camino in meditation.

Thomas, apparently, had had his Bible stolen and now had only an Italian New Testament which wasn't a great deal of use as he had only a sketchy knowledge of Italian.

'Where', asked Thomas The Lawyer, 'could I buy an English Bible in Spain?'

He'd tried unsuccessfully so far.

I said that I doubted that there would be much demand for English Bibles in the small towns of central Spain, where they didn't really cater for passing trade of this sort.

'How about the cathedral shop in Santiago?', I suggested; and Santiago, after all, was where we were all heading and where Thomas had had two Bibles stolen in the past.

Perhaps he might even be able to buy one of them back in a second hand book shop: there was obviously a demand for them there.

Thomas The Lawyer brightened up at this,

I slipped the uneaten bread from the meal into my pocket, for breakfast.

Thomas looked rather shocked: but I'm sure that his keen, analytical mind realised my legal right to the bread following my purchase of a meal. But I still made sure that the waiter didn't see, just in case.

We walked back up the hill to the Refuge: the rain was beginning to settle in.

12

Santiago de Compostela and Home!

Day 38

Arca to Santiago de Compostela

17 km   17 km to go

I'd imagined a luxuriant lie-in on the last morning: 17 km to go according to the Guide Book, and all day to do it!

But it was just like Saint Jean on that first day!

04.00, and people were already creeping from their bunks, banging into each other in the dark, with the insistent rustle of sleeping bags being forced into rucksacks and the pinpricks of torches scouring the dormitory for socks. Whispers got steadily louder: and then the lights went on in the washrooms, and the doors started banging, and the entire section was soon buzzing.

The Young Lady Whose Parents Thought She Was On A Walking Holiday was now alone opposite, swathed in her sheet and breathing deeply, the sleep of the not surprisingly exhausted.

Her Brazilian companion clambered down from the top bunk, and prodded her to get up: he appeared to harbour no resentment.

He was probably just a family friend, keeping an eye on her for the folks back home.

She handed her sheet to him to stuff into his rucksack: within minutes they went off cosily together, shadowy figures turning the corner into the corridor.

0530. Everybody in my eight bed dormitory had gone, and I had the unusual luxury of switching on the light and putting my rucksack on the top bunk to pack.

It was the first time I'd come face to face with a Refuge mattress at close quarters with my glasses on: and I realised that sleeping bags were there not to protect the mattress from the Pilgrim, but the Pilgrim from the mattress.

I won't go into details: but I thought I'd better wash my hands before breakfast.

I pulled on my shorts, which I'd stuffed down my sleeping bag with my bum bag, had a good scratch and wandered into the lobby, packed with gloomy Pilgrims.

The reason for the early start? Thomas The German Named After A Can Of Beer told me that they all wanted to reach Santiago for the midday Mass in the cathedral.

But why the gloom?

'It's raining': the first real rain I had met on the Camino. Was Galicia at last revealing why it was so green?

Pilgrims were shuffling into waterproof ponchos and raintops and trudging out into the dark gloomy morning, rain cascading down their necks from the gutterless roof.

Ponchos looked good: why had I sent mine back from Pamplona and just kept my boil-in-a-bag rain top?

I sat beside Thomas The White Haired Pilgrim From Fatima: he wasn't great company, just sat and meditated.

I cracked open the last of my dry bread, smeared it with a sliver of cheese, drank a cup of water and waited.

I don't like rain. Eight o'clock, and the Hospitalero appeared and ejected me with an experienced smile and a metaphorical arm lock like a civilian Sister Agatha.

Thomas The White Haired Pilgrim From Fatima appeared to have disappeared: he was probably meditating some place where they wouldn't find him until the rain stopped.

Strangely, the rain didn't appear too heavy now it was getting light.

Lorries splashed me as I went up the hard shoulder and turned into the side streets of Arca. A bar owner was guiding wet Pilgrims into his steaming café. Business was booming: it seemed nicely full as I shuffled past.

2 km gone, 15 to go: and I was already on the woodland tracks, with the rain almost stopped.

Half an hour later the rain was torrential: sweat was soaking my shirt and my arms were running with water, as the breathable fabric sorted out whether or not it was going to work. It soon decided. It wasn't.

Up the first long drag: 3 km through the eucalyptus woods before the rain at last stopped.

And that was that! Boil-in-a-bag top off.

I began to dry out: the slope evened out: and it was great walking through the eucalyptus woods.

Santiago airport was somewhere off to the side as I followed the switchback beside the main road and then turned off towards the Monte del Gozo. The kilometre posts had vanished at 12 km: a sure sign that they'd added on a few kilometres to take us off the roads.

The only bar was out of *empanada*: I sorted out my rucksack and then on to Lavacolla. If the guide book says 'a **very** steep hill', prepare to shudder; after all, it's the sort of publication that gets you to 29,000ft on Mt Everest and concludes 'KSO (Keep Straight On) to top of hill'.

Yes, the guide book was **right:** and as usual, once you'd

clawed your way up to the top, and gained a brief respite wandering through the woods, you go **down** again to Lavacolla.

That's where Pilgrims in the Middle Ages washed their clothes and selves before the final stretch into Santiago. Where they dried their bits, I can't imagine: but I guess that they were made of hardier stuff in those days. No wonder half of them never got home.

Lavacolla, therefore, is by the river: and yes, you've guessed it, you can't see Santiago from there so it's obviously over another hill. Over Monte del Gozo (Mount Joy!), in fact: and it's bound to be a good one, you realise, because just before you reach the summit you pass two TV stations. And they put TV stations on top of BIG hills, because the reception's better.

So it was up (with a few downs), past the TV stations, and past the hideous rusting modern statue on top of the mountain itself where you get your first impressive view of Santiago, framed between the banks of the tree lined road.

Soon, you're confronted by the grotesque giant leisure village of Monte del Gozo, which had been just a pleasant green hill before the Pope's visit in 1989. The grey buildings of the 3,000 bed village stretch the length of the hillside, bisected by a swathe of restaurants (closed for lunch), supermarkets, souvenir shops and an amphitheatre.

It looks like a cross between a barracks and a rather forbidding holiday camp.

Pilgrims, apparently, can get a free night's accommodation: but I didn't like to test it.

Don't take my word for it, though: it looks a little too upmarket to welcome sweaty pilgrims unless there's a shed round the back beside the stables.

I thought that I'd get a *sello*, though: so I strolled into the administration office. The elegant young lady behind the desk backed away as I approached, perhaps fearful that she might catch something. She had mastered the art of communication without speech, especially with the more unsavoury visitors: perhaps she hadn't realised that, if it hadn't been for the Pilgrims, the holiday camp (and her job?) wouldn't exist.

'Sello, por favor?' I asked in one of my best one word sentences.

She drew herself up to her full height (well, she was only about 5 ft tall, so she had to, to be able to point effectively) and imperiously pointed to the door and finished with a little twitch to the left. The *sello* and ink pad were on the table outside.

'Bebida (drink)?'

Point to door, **big** twitch to left, and then a crooked finger indicating 'round the corner'.

'Banco?'

She sighed: the free standing hole in the wall (contradiction in terms? Well, **you** know what I mean) was visible from the office, but only accessible from outside.

'Santiago?'

Sign to door, expansive gesture to right towards camp road.

I'd finished: and she lost interest and moved away into an office to reassure herself with her own kind.

I strolled along down the road towards Santiago, thinking that it was a pity that the City Fathers didn't appear to rate the Pilgrims, their original source of income, very highly.

For almost 150 km, I had been ticking off the marker posts with eager anticipation.

Now there were none. Surely these could have been erected all the way over the final 6 km into Santiago and right up to the cathedral as a fitting tribute to the Pilgrims and the Shrine that they were about to visit? There weren't even many yellow arrows: two or three through the entire final 5 km through the depressing suburbs. You couldn't even see the cathedral to get your bearings until you were almost in the square around this most beautiful and imposing building.

At last I felt certain of completing the Camino: even if I fell and broke my leg, at least I could be brought back by ambulance to crawl the remaining hundred metres, although somebody would have to help me up the stairs to get my Compostela!

The squares around the cathedral were packed with Pilgrims, with many of whom I'd shared much of the past five weeks. All smiles, greetings, handshakes: it was like the last day of term!

I was awe struck when I entered the cathedral and sat in the cool seats.

Pilgrims climb the steps at the entrance to the Pórtico de la Gloria, and follow the centuries old tradition of all pilgrims who came before you and place your hands on the Tree of Jesse under the statue of St James. It's hard to imagine how many tens of thousands of hands have worn the stone into it's present shape!

But the focal point of the interior is the 13th century statue of St James above the richly decorated high altar.

You can climb the steps to embrace the statue from behind, another tradition known as 'a hug for the apostle', and then descend under the altar to the shrine of St James with the silver casket in which his remains are said to be kept.

The giant censer, known as the *botafumeiro* because of the clouds of incense that it emits (originally to fumigate the assembled pilgrims!) is always swung on St James' Day, 25th July, and other special feast days.

Pilgrims receive their certificate, their Compostela, on presenting their stamped Pilgrim passport at the Pilgrim Office. The final 100 km of the Camino (from Sarria or Barbadelo) in one continuous stretch for walkers, 200 km for cyclists, is the minimum qualification: a pretty modest requirement, set aside the agonies that Pilgrims had endured in the Middle Ages.

I luxuriated in the slow moving queue, pinned between a group of boy scouts and a squad of cyclists. An imperious gesture beckoned me into the office: and a minute later, I had my Compostela, my certificate!

It was truly one of the great moments of my life.

It was the only major Challenge that I had done entirely on my own: and it was **fantastic**!

Rugby tours might have been challenging and great achievements, but there was always someone looking out for you, making sure that you were alright.

On the Camino, I had been on my own. Nobody knew where I was, or when.

I alone had planned my route, checked into a Refuge, looked after my health, sorted out my food, done my washing and nobody else knew or cared. If I had collapsed, or twisted an ankle, along the Camino, I knew that I could count on help from passing Pilgrims: but there would be nobody at the Refuge that evening to say 'Anybody seen Harry?' and to worry.

So it was one of the great achievements of my life: such a little thing on the world stage, but such a big thing to every individual Pilgrim. I had proved myself: that's why I felt so good!

I had the Compostela laminated and photocopies made. Not at the same shop, of course: that would have been too easy. Up the road, right at the end: a lady who seemed perpetually surprised to be asked for photocopies several hundred times a day.

I ate a shrivelled *empanada*, and having been there, and done that, I bought the T shirt.

At last, I felt entitled to wear the conch shell: and I bought one from the cathedral shop after having sat and offered my thanks before the altar.

I wandered into the Plaza de las Praterias, still wearing my rucksack: there, around the fountain, were fat Juan, Julia and Hermione.

Juan had covered almost 40 km the previous day, to Monte del Gozo, for a short run-in today: Hermione and Julia had arrived by taxi from Ribadiso.

Veronica was chatting animatedly with them, with Michael Fish lookalike José Antonio sagging dispiritedly at her elbow. He had the nervous haunted look of most people who came within Veronica's orbit.

Veronica hadn't liked the rain that morning at Arca, so she also had finished the journey by taxi.

The delectable Charlotte sauntered along. Her stomach, most of which was tantalisingly revealed, was apparently still not quite right: she also had finished the Camino by taxi.

One at least of the four taxi Pilgrims had just been to get their Compostela: no prizes for guessing which.

We took the requisite photographs around the fountain, after which Veronica rounded up escaping Pilgrims and ordered them to attend a celebration meal that evening, meeting at the fountain at 8.30.

She and José Antonio, apparently, had been looking for me: they wanted to take me up to the Refugio at the Seminario which suited me well because I had absolutely no idea where I was going to sleep otherwise.

Thomas, his wife and friend, and the plump Spanish Lady With The American Accent Who Was Living In Essex were also staying there, I remembered.

But first I had to arrange how to get home. Coach seemed the

Santiago at last! Sorry you can't see Juan,
but he's taking the photograph

macho way to do it, a bit of suffering to end with, but coaches to London, via Paris, only went on Sundays and Thursdays and I'd missed it by a day.

But the Travel Agents told me that I could fly to Heathrow, change at Madrid, direct from Santiago the next morning if I wanted! And Iberia offered a substantial discount to Pilgrims with Compostelas!

I could have kissed the plump lady behind the desk: but it might have meant my missing the plane, so I kept myself under control. £132.00 seemed quite cheap, compared with a coach for about £80.00. By the time I met up again with José Antonio and Veronica, who was busy dominating a few more Pilgrims and probably hadn't noticed that I'd even been away, I was grinning from ear to ear.

It was a long trek through uncharted waters to the Seminario. We passed a few more Pilgrims lolling outside various bars on the way: all were ordered to be at the fountain at 8.30.

The Seminario looked like one of the grimmer Victorian prisons, high on a hill overlooking Santiago.

The big gates were now open and they'd taken the broken glass and barbed wire off the top of the walls, although the security lights were still in place: but even so, escape seemed pretty difficult.

We were in the long dormitory on the third floor: beds as well as bunks, lots of spare pillows, luxury! I grabbed a bed: I still hadn't got into the habit of diving for the bottom bunk and then sitting hunched up in agony, moaning, after raking my head on the pointed springs of the top bunk whenever I stood up suddenly.

Showers? Fourth floor: unfortunately, some students had taken the equipment out of those in our dormitory. Toilets: they'd done the same to those, also, apart from the ones they'd blocked up. Ah well, students will be students, I suppose.

Final Chapter

It was too late for a shower: nowhere to dry my towel before tomorrow.

So I used my roll-on deodorant fairly lavishly and shaved (Ada's razor was standing up to this regular every-five-day regime splendidly, and I'd thrown in an extra session the previous day out of deference to my imminent visit to the cathedral).

Veronica materialised at my elbow.

'Will you be ready by eight o'clock?' We got ready to leave shortly after 8.30. I thought that all the Pilgrims would be waiting eagerly at the fountain by then.

'Oh, this is **Spain**' murmured Veronica, resplendent in clean short shorts and yet **another** off the shoulder top.

There were big warnings about being on your guard against theft, in this religious Seminario in the Holy City of Santiago de Compostela: of **course**, Santiago was where Thomas The White Haired Pilgrim From Fatima had had a couple of Bibles nicked in the past!

I packed everything into the locker beside the bed: but as it had no lock, it didn't seem to serve much purpose. Anyway, they didn't like untidy Pilgrims leaving their rucksacks on the floor and their belongings on the bed, so I might as well go with the tide!

But I kept my valuables strapped round my waist, as usual.

We'd got halfway to the fountain before we met a group of Pilgrims who Veronica had failed to round up earlier. Unfortunately, they couldn't come to the meal: but they got a stern pep talk.

We reached the fountain by 9.

Juan, Julia and Hermione were lurking on a corner: a long conversation ensued.

José Antonio stood uncomfortably in the background, looking as Michael Fish must have looked the morning after he found out that the gusty winds promised by the Met. Office the previous evening had turned into the biggest storm to hit Southern England since – well, we don't know since **when**, because it was before we began keeping records of that sort of thing.

I had a chat with him, as we were both apparently excluded from the discussion. He'd been on an English speaking course in Tonbridge fifteen years ago, so felt a certain empathy with East Grinstead (probably because I told him it was almost a **suburb** of Tonbridge, to engage his interest)

I was getting hungry. I hadn't eaten since my dry bread that morning, and my shrivelled *empanada* at midday. I told him that I was going to find a restaurant and I'd make my own way back to the Seminario.

He took the news stoically.

The only bars I visited didn't do meals: and I was soon lost (what's new?) and had no idea how to find my way back to the Seminario. So I retraced my steps. They were all still there: Veronica hadn't noticed I'd gone, so I started to make hungry noises.

'Manolos!' said Veronica. Juan and his ladies made their escape into the dark side streets. The party had been reduced to the organiser and her pressganged crew.

So we went to Casa Manolo, the most popular restaurant in town: three courses with bread and water for €5.5. It was very full (well, it would be, at £3.50 for a good three course meal in the centre of, say, Manchester, wouldn't it?). The proprietor was making gloomy noises about being full when Veronica suddenly saw three escaped Pilgrims at a large table in the corner, the two voluptuous Spanish Girls From Down South and the English Teacher.

They'd been shuffled up and room made in no time.

The girls were eager to speak English: so the entire table spoke **my** language. It was great!

'Do you speak any Spanish?' murmured Juanita, struggling to escape from her restraining blouse and dark eyes flashing.

'Oh, bits: you know, bocadillo, café con leche grande...'

'What about cama (bed)?' she teased.

'...donde, aqui, hoy, cuanto cuesta, mercado...' I continued desperately.

'Would you **like** to speak Spanish, Harry?' asked Veronica.

'Well, I wouldn't mind'.

'I could teach you', she said. 'Do you live by yourself'?'

'No, no, I... er... live with my son and his family, and in any case I'm never there, I'm always away, and I don't think that Spanish would **really** be of great use...'

Fortunately, the first course arrived then: a particularly insipid Galician potato soup, which I'd only ordered because I thought that it was time I sampled more local dishes, with my going home tomorrow, and I didn't fancy paella, rubbery squid, or octopus.

This was followed by an enormous steak and chips: then a tray of seven yoghourts was thrust on to the table (one spare? They'd miscounted: and I was about to shove the extra one into my pocket for breakfast until I realised that this was no longer necessary).

'Let's have a celebration drink' said the party organiser (you don't really want me to tell you who **this** was, do you?): and off we went to a small empty bar off the Plaza del Obradoiro, where the proprietor was probably hoping for an early night and thinking of closing early.

Café con leche and then… what was it? A pale yellow liqueur which tasted like grappa and had the kick of an angry horse.

Cameras out. José Antonio and the barman were pressed into service.

'Let's go and listen to the Tuna!' (a musical group made up of University students, not the fish) cried Veronica, probably to the relief of the barman, who'd unfortunately just gained another customer who wasn't going to improve the family fortunes substantially with her order for one black coffee.

We'd scarcely got out of the door before Veronica found someone with whom to talk.

We waited… and waited. The Spanish Girls From Down South flushed her out by shouting 'Good night, Veronica', at which she came running along.

The Tuna, a group of student musicians in mediaeval dress playing their own catchy Spanish style music with (saucy?) lyrics, had gathered a huge crowd: the girls gyrated enthusiastically, after Veronica had greeted more friends, whilst José Antonio and myself stood, English style, at the back. I resisted the temptation to buy one of their CDs, which were being hawked round. Perhaps next time, I consoled myself later: or, if they had a website, I might be able to copy it **free**.

No, no, no: forget I said **that**!

I kept looking at my watch. The doors of the Seminario were locked at midnight.

Did this mean Spanish or English midnight?

'Half past eleven, Veronica' I said, worried.

'OK, five minutes, they'll soon be finished'.

'Quarter to twelve'

'Yes, OK'.

Finally, I faced her and said, sternly, 'It's thirteen minutes to midnight, and it's more than ten minutes to the Seminario, and we're going'.

I dragged the reluctant José Antonio along as Veronica continued to gyrate enthusiastically with the Spanish Girls From Down South (**they** were alright, they'd got rooms in a Hostal and their own key) and began to stride it out towards the Seminario.

'Spanish people like to dance and party until late at night in the summer,' puffed José Antonio: 'but, me, I am not typical and I like to go home early'.

I warmed to him: we could have settled for a bocadillo at a local bar and a café con leche grande instead. He was a man after my own heart, a Horlicks and book at bedtime man: what were we doing racing round a remote Spanish city, seduced (metaphorically speaking) by the dominant Veronica?

As we rounded the corner of the Seminario, the cathedral clock began to strike midnight. Where was the door?

Round the next corner.

I got round the next corner. Where was the door?

'Round the **next** corner' puffed José Antonio, now several yards off the pace.

Two minutes past midnight: and we tumbled in through the enormous doors which probably took a squad of several men to close.

The Hospitalero was still behind his desk: the Italian students still hadn't got back, let alone Veronica, and he wasn't going to wait much longer.

We'd been to see the Tuna, we told him.

'I **hate** the Tuna' he roared, galvanised into activity.

'They're rich students, who do no work, and the words of their songs are not … er … nice: and we poor students work hard and get **nothing**.'

I didn't think it the right time or place to comment that, actually, I thought they were rather good: as the *News of the World* used to put at the bottom of their more salacious investigative reports, 'Our reporter made his apologies and left'.

I was in bed and asleep in no time: I quickly dismissed any fleeting worries that I might have about Veronica, alone in a strange city. She'd probably sleep on the floor at the Hostal where the Spanish Girls From Down South were staying.

I woke at 6.30. Veronica was packing.

Just got in, I thought smugly.

I wandered along for a wash an hour later, hoping that the students hadn't pinched more of the plumbing in the past twelve hours.

Veronica, with José Antonio in tow, appeared at my elbow.

The Tuna had finished a few minutes later, and she'd set off back to the Seminario, lost her way, and called in at a bar that was closing to persuade the last client to take her back to the Seminario. Probably too scared to resist.

'I arrived at 12.45. It was closed, and I have never been so frightened in all my life, thinking of sleeping alone at night outside this building. I called, and José came down to open the door for me. He is my angel,' she cooed.

José Antonio smiled modestly. Apparently, he had been too worried to sleep.

Relationships between the three of us appeared to have cooled.

'We are going to find a café and have breakfast' summed up Veronica 'before we catch our trains at 9 o'clock.'

I said goodbye. We seemed to lack the empathy that had formerly existed: and they trailed off down the dormitory.

I packed, put on my rucksack, went down the three flights of stairs and set off, walking down the road and then up the long steep hill to the bus station to get the bus to the airport and home.

I looked up to the sky and blew a kiss. 'Thank you, darling, for holding my hand'.

Was it Successful?

How do you measure success?

It was a great experience, one that I wouldn't want to have missed: it was one of the experiences of a lifetime.

True, it didn't raise much money for Myfanwy's Charity.

I was sponsored for a total of £112.50; if I hadn't paid all my expenses, it would have lost money!

But it was a **Pilgrimage,** in every sense of the word: and I gained so much from it in every way.

It also proved that my planned walk from end to end of New Zealand in early 2004, pushing a wheelbarrow, was definitely feasible.

Why a wheelbarrow? To raise 'a wheelbarrow full of money', of course: read all about it in *Harry the Wheelbarrow Man*.

So **yes**, it was a resounding success: and it was enriched by all the people that I met along the way.